BABYLON BURNING

**A GRAPHIC HISTORY OF THE MAKING OF
THE MODERN MIDDLE EAST**

TOUFIC EL RASSI

LAST GASP
SAN FRANCISCO

Babylon Burning

Written and drawn by Toufic El Rassi

Inks and graphic design by Elizabeth Hamilton

Edited and designed by Colin Turner

Special thanks to:
The School of the Art Institute of Chicago
Richard El Rassi
Lilian Jimenez
Desi Swain
Honey Bennet
Candida Alvarez
Hollace Graff
Last Gasp
The Low Residency MFA Program at
the School of the Art Institute of Chicago
Gregg Bordowitz
The Academic Advising Office at
the School of the Art Institute of Chicago
Rebekah Champ
Eric Lebofsky
The Continuing Studies Program at
the School of the Art Institute of Chicago
Kristina Wyatt

Dedicated to Rasmea Odeh

Published by
Last Gasp of San Francisco
777 Florida Street
San Francisco, CA 94110
www.lastgasp.com

ISBN 978-0-86719-866-9
First Trade Edition, March 2019
Printed in China

INTRODUCTION

When I started Babylon Burning in the wake of my first book (Arab in America) I thought I would be able to finish relatively quickly. I was wrong. Aside from some personal obstacles, I didn't appreciate the task I had undertaken. In other words: I bit off more than I could chew. Researching the history of US involvement in the Middle East was challenging. Over the years the project came to include more than just the Middle East, and that made it even more unwieldy. I also had to draw the pictures, which was considerably more fun than the research. After being asked countless times: "when is your next book coming out?" I can finally give an answer.

This book is the end result of a youth involved in activism, and an aborted pursuit of a PhD in Middle Eastern studies. Even though my politics and worldview have changed over the years, I was adamant about finishing this book.

I thought about why my parents moved to the US from Beirut. All I knew was what I saw on TV, it was a place of violence, fanaticism, instability, and underdevelopment. In college, I learned the history of western and US involvement in the region. That history went a long way to explain the troubles of the area. It is a history that is often ignored, or underappreciated, and is not easily accessible to many people.

I remember being upset by news reports and stories from the media that failed to contextualize events in the Middle East. I still have trouble watching coverage of the Middle East without wincing.

Corporate media is often biased, and Babylon Burning is meant to be a challenge to the dominant narrative. I do not claim objectivity in my presentation—I inject my political beliefs. I also do not claim that the United States or the West is the sole reason for the troubles in the Middle East, but they share a significant responsibility for the situation.

It is hard to imagine what the Middle East would look like today had it not been for continuous US and European involvement in the region.

Because of petroleum, and other geopolitical concerns, it's not likely foreign powers will cease meddling in the region anytime soon. This sad reality makes Babylon Burning more relevant than ever. I hope it will help readers in their quest to more clearly understand this unstable and critical part of the world.

Toufic El Rassi

Chicago

January 2017

BABYLON BURNING

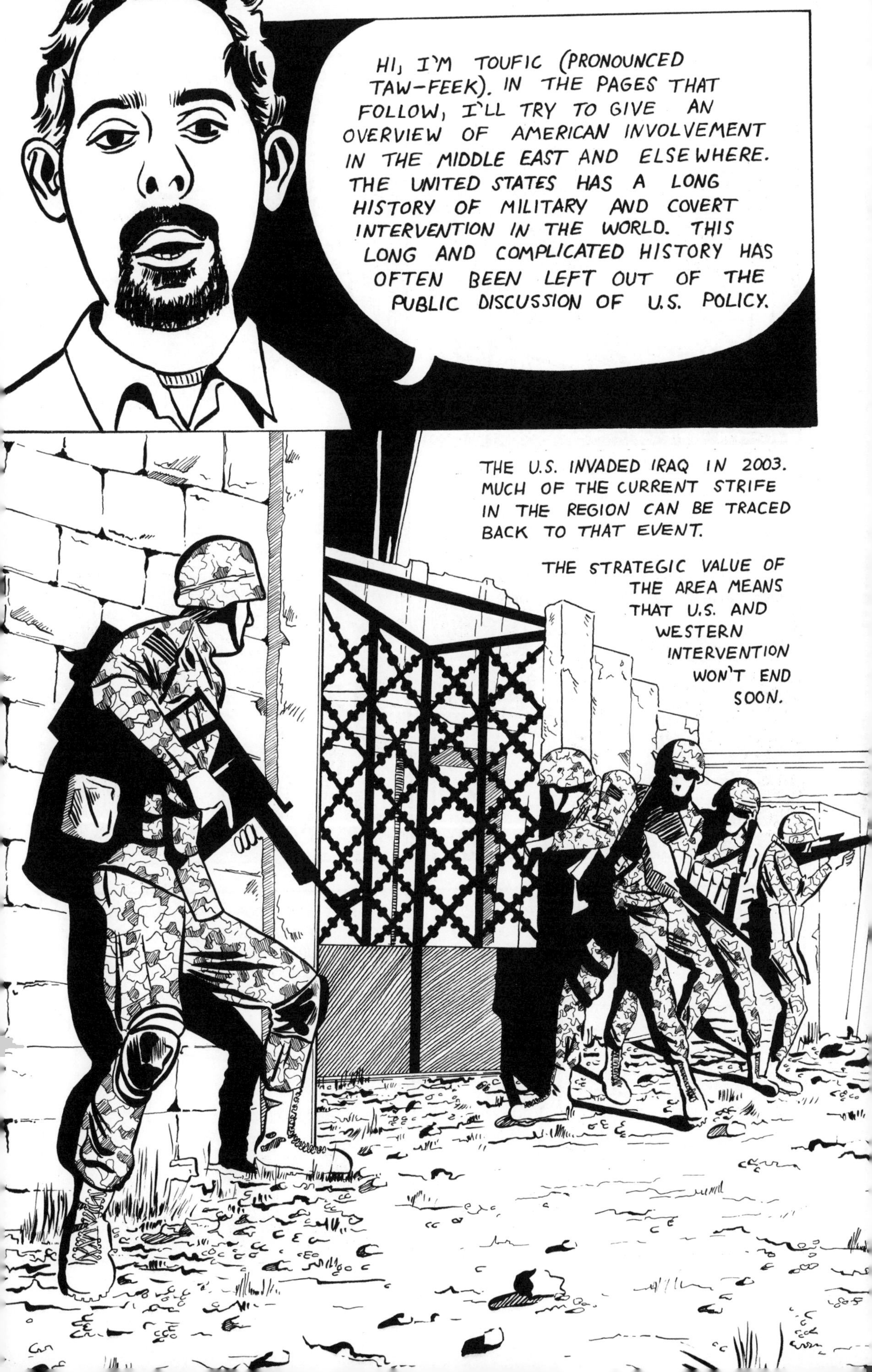
HI, I'M TOUFIC (PRONOUNCED TAW-FEEK). IN THE PAGES THAT FOLLOW, I'LL TRY TO GIVE AN OVERVIEW OF AMERICAN INVOLVEMENT IN THE MIDDLE EAST AND ELSEWHERE. THE UNITED STATES HAS A LONG HISTORY OF MILITARY AND COVERT INTERVENTION IN THE WORLD. THIS LONG AND COMPLICATED HISTORY HAS OFTEN BEEN LEFT OUT OF THE PUBLIC DISCUSSION OF U.S. POLICY.
THE U.S. INVADED IRAQ IN 2003. MUCH OF THE CURRENT STRIFE IN THE REGION CAN BE TRACED BACK TO THAT EVENT.
THE STRATEGIC VALUE OF THE AREA MEANS THAT U.S. AND WESTERN INTERVENTION WON'T END SOON.

SUFFICE IT TO SAY, THE RELATIONSHIP BETWEEN THE WEST & THE MIDDLE EAST HAS BEEN AN UNEQUAL ONE SINCE THE DAYS OF EUROPEAN COLONIALISM.

IN MY CAPACITY AS A PROFESSOR, I'VE GAINED VALUABLE INSIGHT INTO THE WAY MANY AMERICANS VIEW THE MIDDLE EAST.

AS AN ARAB LIVING IN THE UNITED STATES, I FEEL LIKE I GET TO SEE U.S. POLICIES & HISTORY WITHOUT ROSE-COLORED GLASSES. I'M FORCED TO THINK ABOUT U.S. FOREIGN POLICY IN A WAY MOST AMERICANS DON'T CONSIDER.

SO MY OPINIONS & PERSPECTIVES ARE OFTEN AT ODDS WITH THE MAINSTREAM.

AS YOUR HUMBLE GUIDE, I'LL TRY TO LAYOUT THE OFTEN UNKNOWN & DEEPLY TROUBLING POLICIES & HISTORY OF THE U.S., BOTH AT HOME & ABROAD.

I HOPE THIS BOOK WILL SHED SOME LIGHT ON THE ANGER & DISTRUST THAT MANY PEOPLE HAVE TOWARDS AMERICAN POLICIES, & SERVE AS A DOCUMENT OF SORTS. LET'S START WITH AN OVERVIEW OF THE MIDDLE EAST

THIS PERENNIALLY VOLATILE REGION SEEMS TO BE AS CHAOTIC AS EVER, ESPECIALLY WITH THE MOVEMENTS THAT OVERTHREW MANY REGIMES BEGINNING IN 2011...

AND THE BRUTAL WAR IN SYRIA...

AND THE RISE OF ARMED ISLAMIC GROUPS THROUGHOUT THE AREA...

AND THE TENSION OVER IRAN'S NUCLEAR PROGRAM...

AND THE NEVER-ENDING ISRAELI / PALESTINIAN CONFLICT...

AND THE CONSTANT INTERFERENCE OF THE UNITED STATES...

AS THE BIRTHPLACE OF CIVILIZATION, THE MIDDLE EAST HAS A LONG HISTORY OF UPHEAVAL, CONQUEST, TRANSFORMATION, AND WAR...

BUT THE MOST RECENT SERIES OF UPHEAVALS COULD ARGUABLY BE TRACED BACK TO THE U.S. INVASION OF IRAQ IN 2003.

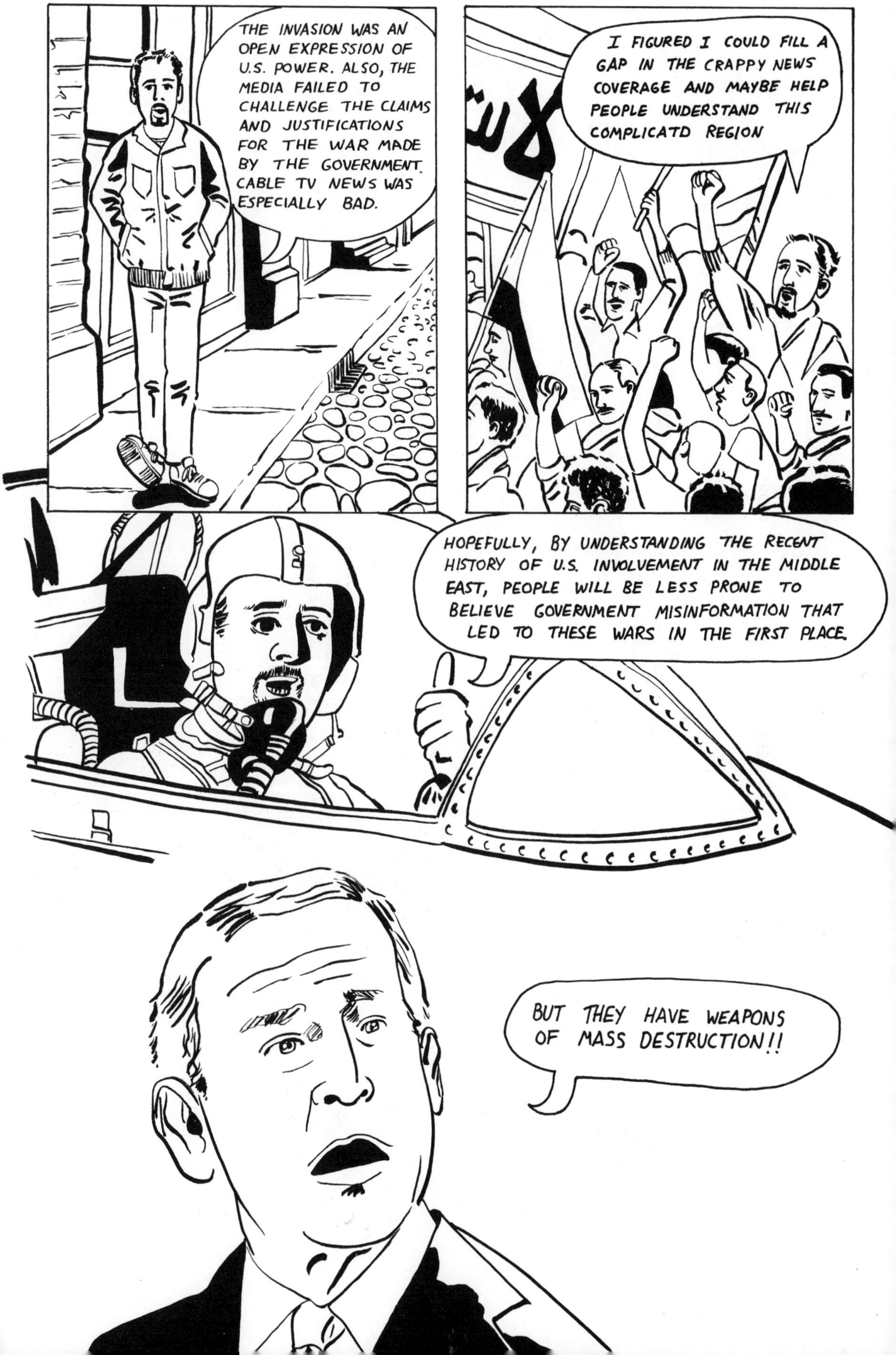
THE INVASION WAS AN OPEN EXPRESSION OF U.S. POWER. ALSO, THE MEDIA FAILED TO CHALLENGE THE CLAIMS AND JUSTIFICATIONS FOR THE WAR MADE BY THE GOVERNMENT. CABLE TV NEWS WAS ESPECIALLY BAD.
I FIGURED I COULD FILL A GAP IN THE CRAPPY NEWS COVERAGE AND MAYBE HELP PEOPLE UNDERSTAND THIS COMPLICATD REGION
HOPEFULLY, BY UNDERSTANDING THE RECENT HISTORY OF U.S. INVOLVEMENT IN THE MIDDLE EAST, PEOPLE WILL BE LESS PRONE TO BELIEVE GOVERNMENT MISINFORMATION THAT LED TO THESE WARS IN THE FIRST PLACE.
BUT THEY HAVE WEAPONS OF MASS DESTRUCTION!!

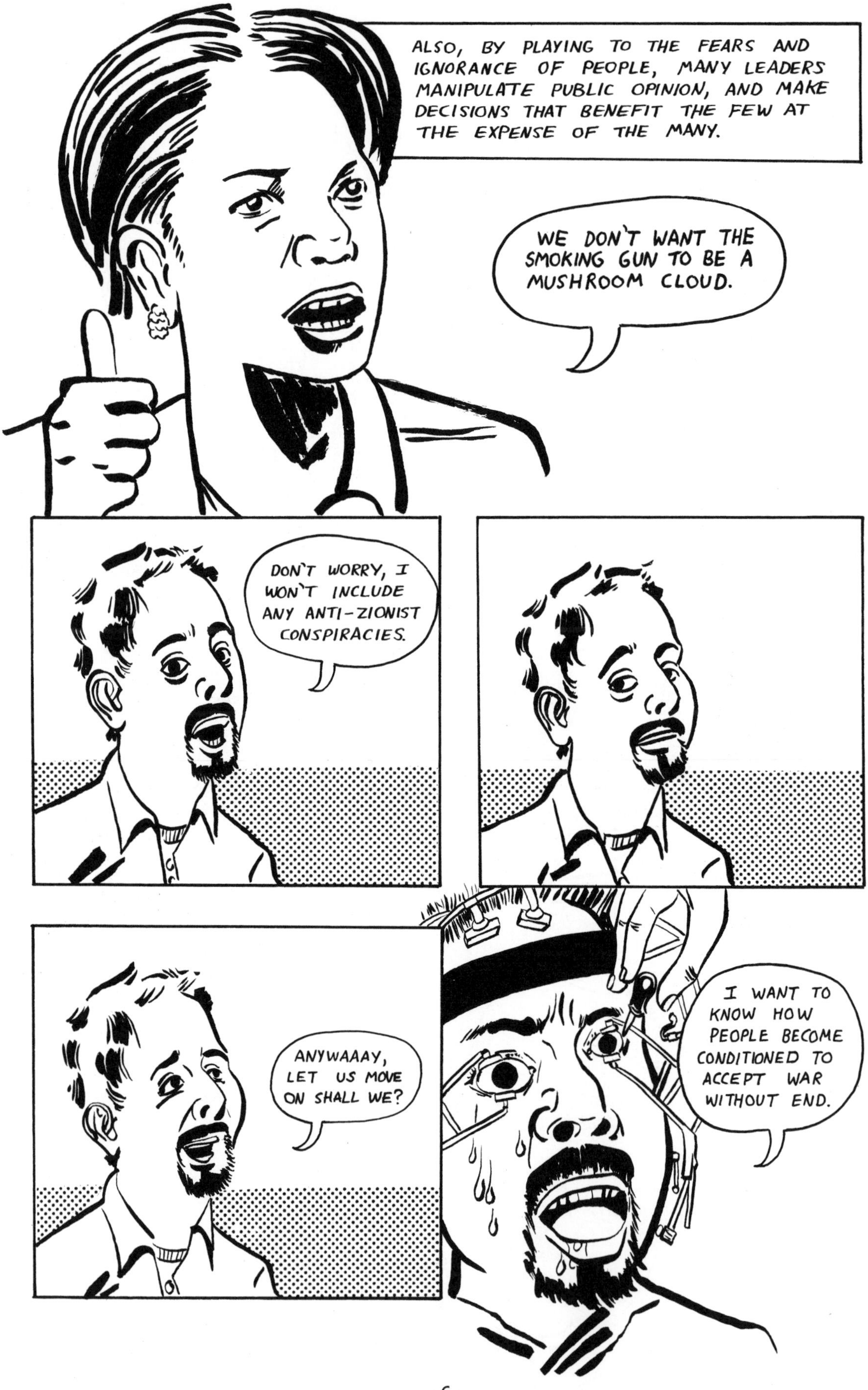
ALSO, BY PLAYING TO THE FEARS AND IGNORANCE OF PEOPLE, MANY LEADERS MANIPULATE PUBLIC OPINION, AND MAKE DECISIONS THAT BENEFIT THE FEW AT THE EXPENSE OF THE MANY.
WE DON'T WANT THE SMOKING GUN TO BE A MUSHROOM CLOUD.
DON'T WORRY, I WON'T INCLUDE ANY ANTI-ZIONIST CONSPIRACIES.
ANYWAAAY, LET US MOVE ON SHALL WE?
I WANT TO KNOW HOW PEOPLE BECOME CONDITIONED TO ACCEPT WAR WITHOUT END.

LEADERS WHO SEEK PUBLIC SUPPORT FOR THEIR POLICIES EXPLOIT THE FEAR OF TERRORISM, BUT THE REALITY OF THE THREAT IS AT ODDS WITH THE MEDIA-HYPED NARRATIVE.

MOST VICTIMS ARE MUSLIM AND ACCOUNT FOR 82-97 PERCENT OF TERRORISM-RELATED FATALITIES (2012) - OF 13,288 KILLED IN 2011, 17 WERE PRIVATE U.S. CITIZENS.[1]

A COMPARABLE NUMBER OF AMERICANS ARE CRUSHED TO DEATH BY THEIR TELEVISIONS OR FURNITURE.[2]

UNTIL THE MASS KILLINGS IN MIAMI AND SAN BERNADINO CA, THERE WERE NOT MANY ISLAMIC INSPIRED ATTACKS IN THE USA.

SINCE 9/11, UNTIL 2015, 1 PERCENT OF 14,000 MURDERS IN THE U.S. WERE A RESULT OF TERRORISM.[3]

AND THAT IS USING THE MEDIA'S DEFINITION OF TERRORISM.

26 MURDERS WERE A RESULT OF DOMESTIC RIGHT WING TERRORISTS.[4]

WHY DO THE MEDIA ONLY LABEL MURDERS ASSOCIATED WITH ISLAM "TERRORISM?"

DO YOU SUPPORT ISIS?

Don Lemon

LIVE CNN

ACCORDING TO THE NEW AMERICA FOUNDATION, WHITE AMERICANS ARE THE BIGGEST TERROR THREAT IN THE UNITED STATES.[5]

ALONG WITH RADICAL ANTI-GOVERNMENT GROUPS, WHITE SUPREMACISTS ARE ALSO PERPETRATORS OF POLITICALLY MOTIVATED VIOLENCE.

A NEO NAZI KILLED 6 PEOPLE IN 2012 AT A SIKH TEMPLE IN WISCONSIN.

IN LAS VEGAS, A WHITE SUPREMACIST COUPLE KILLED 2 COPS & 1 CIVILIAN IN A WAL-MART PARKING LOT. THEY LEFT A FLAG OF A SWASTIKA & A GADSDEN FLAG ON THE BODIES. THEY ALSO LEFT A NOTE SAYING: "THIS IS THE BEGINNING OF THE REVOLUTION."

IN THE PACIFIC NORTHWEST, 2 WHITE RACISTS WENT ON A SHOOTING SPREE IN 2011. THEY KILLED 4 PEOPLE.[6]

STILL NO WHITE AMERICANS IN GUANTANAMO THOUGH.

A WORD ABOUT TERRORISM; THIS WORD HAS PRACTICALLY LOST ITS MEANING TODAY. IT SEEMS THAT "TERRORISM" IS ONLY "TERRORISM" IF A MUSLIM IS INVOLVED SOMEHOW.

BREAKING NEWS

AFTER A MASS SHOOTING, SOMETHING REPORTERS OFTEN SAY EARLY ON IS:

WE DON'T KNOW IF IT'S TERRORISM YET!

NAVY SECRETARY RAY MABUS SAID:

WE EXPECT OUR SAILORS & MARINES TO GO INTO HARM'S WAY, & THEY DO SO WITHOUT HESITATION, AN ATTACK AT HOME, IN OUR COMMUNITY, IS INSIDIOUS AND UNFATHOMABLE.[7]

HE PEN

I MEAN, HOW DO WE KNOW IF IT'S "TERRORISM?" IS THERE A TERRORIST DETECTOR? WHAT WOULD IT LOOK LIKE?

TERROR

BEEP

BEEP

TERROR

BUZZ

NO TERROR

AMERICA ACTUALLY DOES HAVE DEFINITIONS OF "TERRORISM." FOR EXAMPLE, TITLE 22, SEC 2656 OF THE U.S. CODE SAYS IT'S "PREMEDITATED, POLITICALLY MOTIVATED VIOLENCE PERPETRATED AGAINST NONCOMBATANT TARGETS."[7]

THE KEY BIT THERE IS "NON-COMBATANT." SO, ATTACKING SOLDIERS IS WAR, BUT KILLING CIVILIANS IS TERRORISM. (NO MATTER WHO DOES IT.)[8]

MOHAMMOD YOUSSUF ABDULAZEEZ KILLED 4 SOLDIERS IN CHATTANOOGA, TENNESSEE IN JULY 2015.

IN NOVEMBER 2009, NIDAL MALIK HASAN, A U.S. ARMY MAJOR, KILLED SOLDIERS - NOT CIVILIANS.

HASAN

U.S.A.

LET'S KEEP THAT IN MIND NEXT TIME A DRONE ATTACK IN AFGHANISTAN OR PAKISTAN RESULTS IN "COLLATERAL DAMAGE."

OOPS!

E PENTAGON

HISTORIAN GABRIEL KOLKO SAID:

WARFARE AFTER 1937 HAS INCREASINGLY ELIMINATED THE DISTINCTION BETWEEN COMBATANTS & OTHERS... TRAUMATIZING MORE & MORE CIVILIANS & ENTIRE NATIONS.[9]

35 MILLION PEOPLE HAVE BEEN KILLED SINCE WWII IN 170 WARS. 90 PERCENT WERE CIVILIANS.[10]

FOR EXAMPLE, 3.8 MILLION PEOPLE WERE KILLED IN THE VIETNAM WAR. MOST WERE CIVILIANS.[11]

ESTIMATES OF CIVILIAN DEATHS FROM THE 1991 GULF WAR RANGE FROM 100,000 TO 200,000.[12]

AND SINCE THE 2003 INVASION OF IRAQ: BETWEEN 140,000 AND 160,000 CIVILIANS WERE KILLED.[13]

WE DON'T DO BODY COUNTS.

GEORGE ORWELL WROTE:

WHO CONTROLS THE PAST CONTROLS THE FUTURE. WHO CONTROLS THE PRESENT CONTROLS THE PAST.

HE WAS DESCRIBING A DYSTOPIAN FUTURE WHERE PEOPLE WERE LIED TO BY A TOTALITARIAN STATE.

BIG BROTHER WATCHING YO

IN A TIME OF UNIVERSAL DECEIT — TELLING THE TRUTH IS A REVOLUTIONARY ACT.

WITH THE RISE OF FOX NEWS, AND THE CONCENTRATION OF MEDIA CONTROL...

FOX NEWS

AND DESPITE ACCESS TO INFORMATION ON AN UNPRECEDENTED SCALE, IT IS HARD TO BELIEVE THE GOVERNMENT-MEDIA AXIS CAN CREATE PUBLIC AQUIESCENCE OF CONTINUOUS WAR.

POLITICAL LANGUAGE IS DESIGNED TO MAKE LIES SOUND TRUTHFUL AND MURDER RESPECTABLE, AND TO GIVE AN APPEARANCE OF SOLIDITY TO PURE WIND.

INGSOL

INGSO

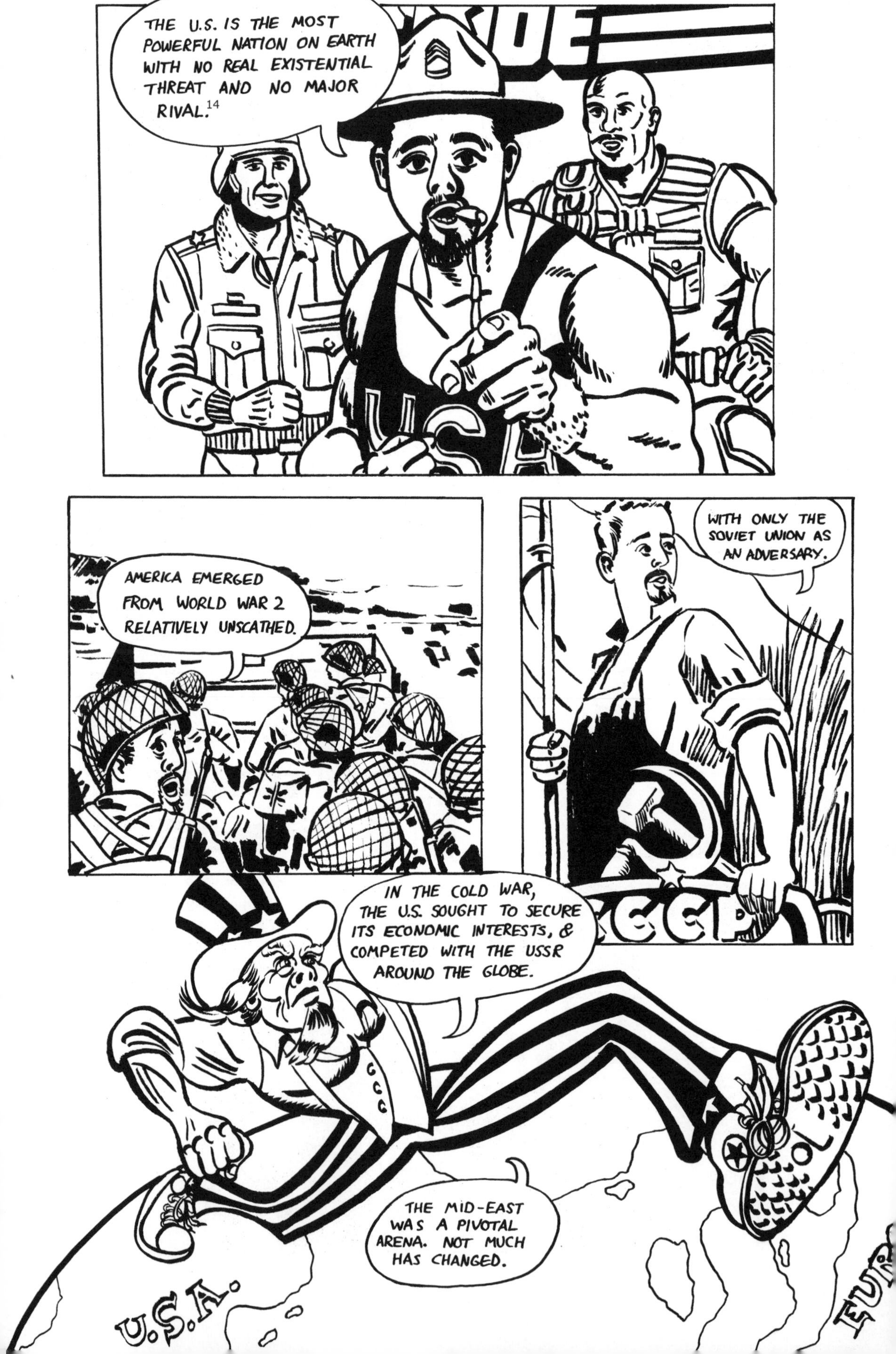
THE U.S. IS THE MOST POWERFUL NATION ON EARTH WITH NO REAL EXISTENTIAL THREAT AND NO MAJOR RIVAL.[14]
AMERICA EMERGED FROM WORLD WAR 2 RELATIVELY UNSCATHED.
WITH ONLY THE SOVIET UNION AS AN ADVERSARY.
IN THE COLD WAR, THE U.S. SOUGHT TO SECURE ITS ECONOMIC INTERESTS, & COMPETED WITH THE USSR AROUND THE GLOBE.
THE MID-EAST WAS A PIVOTAL ARENA. NOT MUCH HAS CHANGED.
U.S.A.

WITH THE THREAT OF AL QAEDA, IT WAS EASIER TO CONVINCE A FRIGHTENED PUBLIC THAT WAR WAS NECESSARY.

WITH NATIONALISM STOKED AND PATRIOTISM VERGING ON JINGOISM, WAR WAS INEVITABLE.

WE'RE GOING TO ATTACK SOMEBODY. WE'RE GOING TO BOMB SOMEPLACE, THERE IS NO QUESTION ABOUT THAT. THE QUESTION IS WHERE & WHY.

AMERICA'S NEW WAR

BEFORE THE INVASION OF IRAQ, A FRIEND ASKED ME:

WHERE IS I-RACK ANYWAY?

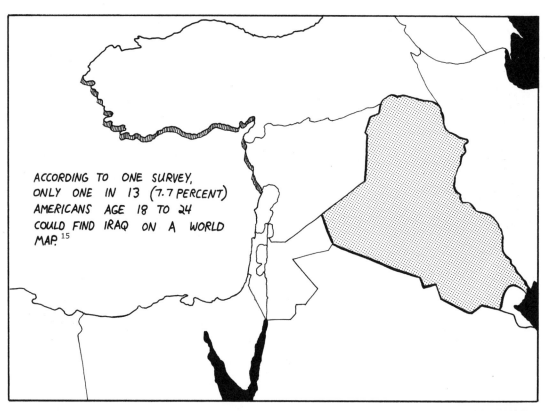

ACCORDING TO ONE SURVEY, ONLY ONE IN 13 (7.7 PERCENT) AMERICANS AGE 18 TO 24 COULD FIND IRAQ ON A WORLD MAP. [15]

MANY AMERICANS EVEN HAVE MUCH DIFFICULTY IDENTIFYING THE "ENEMY."

ARABS?

MUSLIMS?

AL QAEDA?

ISLAMO-FASCISM?

THE U.S. IS AS INVOLVED IN THE MID-EAST AS EVER, WITH ATTACKS ON MUSLIM GROUPS THAT EMERGED AFTER THE INVASION OF IRAQ AND THE SYRIAN REVOLUTION.

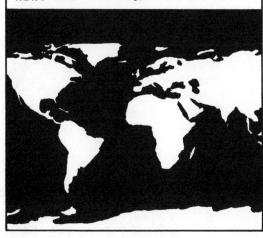

BUT 50 PERCENT OF AMERICANS COULDN'T FIND SYRIA ON A MAP EITHER.[16]

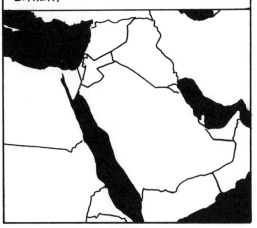

ONLY 3 OUT OF 10 THINK IT'S NECESSARY TO KNOW WHERE COUNTRIES IN THE NEWS ARE LOCATED.[17]

SADLY, 41 PERCENT OF AMERICANS THINK DINOSAURS & MEN LIVED AT THE SAME TIME.[18]

8 IN 10 BELIEVE IN THE EXISTENCE OF ANGELS.[19]

AND 6 PERCENT BELIEVE IN UNICORNS ACCORDING TO A STUDY.[20]

AND EVEN AFTER ALL THESE YEARS, MANY STILL WONDER WHY U.S. SOLDIERS HAVE BEEN SENT TO KILL AND DIE IN THIS VOLATILE REGION. ACCORDING TO GEORGE BUSH AND OTHERS, THERE ARE A NUMBER OF REASONS:

BECAUSE IRAQ WAS DEVELOPING WEAPONS OF MASS DESTRUCTION.

BECAUSE IT'S A BATTLE AGAINST TERRORISM AND ISLAMIC FUNDAMENTALISM.

BECAUSE THEY HATE OUR WAY OF LIFE, AND OUR FREEDOM.

BECAUSE WE WANT TO SPREAD DEMOCRACY IN THE MIDDLE EAST.

AND ACCORDING TO A POLL TAKEN IN SEPTEMBER 2003, SEVEN IN 10 AMERICANS BELIEVED THAT SADDAM HUSSEIN PLAYED A ROLE IN THE 911 ATTACKS. MANY AMERICANS RATIONALIZED THE WAR ON THAT BASIS.[21]

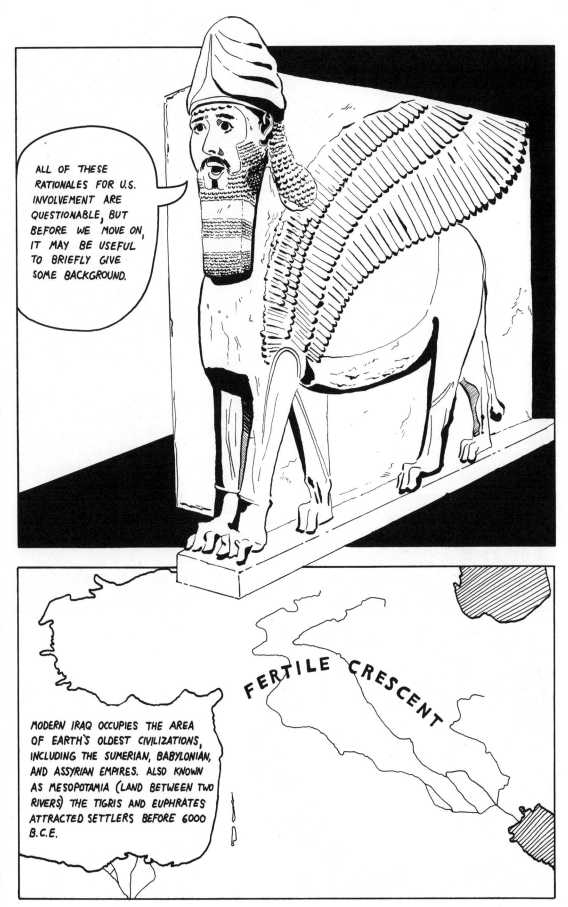

ALL OF THESE RATIONALES FOR U.S. INVOLVEMENT ARE QUESTIONABLE, BUT BEFORE WE MOVE ON, IT MAY BE USEFUL TO BRIEFLY GIVE SOME BACKGROUND.

FERTILE CRESCENT

MODERN IRAQ OCCUPIES THE AREA OF EARTH'S OLDEST CIVILIZATIONS, INCLUDING THE SUMERIAN, BABYLONIAN, AND ASSYRIAN EMPIRES. ALSO KNOWN AS MESOPOTAMIA (LAND BETWEEN TWO RIVERS) THE TIGRIS AND EUPHRATES ATTRACTED SETTLERS BEFORE 6000 B.C.E.

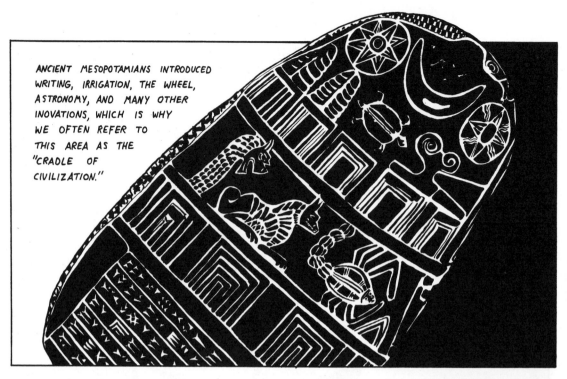

ANCIENT MESOPOTAMIANS INTRODUCED WRITING, IRRIGATION, THE WHEEL, ASTRONOMY, AND MANY OTHER INOVATIONS, WHICH IS WHY WE OFTEN REFER TO THIS AREA AS THE "CRADLE OF CIVILIZATION."

THE BABYLONIAN KING HAMMURABI INTRODUCED ONE OF THE EARLIEST CODES OF LAW, KNOWN AS "THE CODE OF HAMMURABI," IN THE EARLY 18TH CENTURY B.C.E.

FROM 2000 B.C.E., UNTIL 650 A.C.E., IRAQ WAS ALTERNATELY RULED BY THE HITTITES, ASSYRIANS, CHALDEANS, PERSIANS, AND EVEN BY ALEXANDER THE GREAT IN THE 330s B.C.E.

OBVIOUSLY, THIS LAND IS FULL OF SOME OF THE WORLD'S MOST IMPORTANT ARCHEOLOGICAL SITES AND TREASURES. THE NATIONAL MUSEUM OF IRAQ IN BAGHDAD HAD FEW RIVALS WHEN IT CAME TO ITS COLLECTION.

WE ALL WITNESSED THE TRAGEDY IN THE WAKE OF THE UNITED STATES' INVASION IN 2003 WHEN THE MUSEUM WAS LOOTED AND ABOUT 15,000 ARTIFACTS WERE STOLEN.[22]

THIS IVORY SCULPTURE FROM 800 B.C.E IS ONE OF THE MANY ITEMS STILL MISSING.[23]

THIS EIGHTH CENTURY B.C.E PIECE, NAMED "LIONESS ATTACKING A NUBIAN BOY" IS ANOTHER MISSING ARTIFACT.[24]

A LIFE SIZED TERRA COTTA LION STATUE, WHICH ONCE GUARDED THE TEMPLE AT TELL HARMAL DURING THE OLD BABYLONIAN PERIOD, CIRCA 1800 B.C.E., SITS DAMAGED AFTER LOOTERS SACKED THE NATIONAL MUSEUM.[25]

THE LOSSES AND DAMAGE SUFFERED ARE INCALCULABLE, ESPECIALLY BECAUSE THIS IS MORE THAN IRAQ'S HERITAGE, BUT THE WORLD'S.

THE MIDDLE EAST WAS DIVIDED BETWEEN THE WESTERN BYZANTINE EMPIRE, AND THE EASTERN SASANIAN EMPIRE, WHICH WERE AT WAR WITH EACH OTHER WHEN IN 636 A.C.E., AFTER THE INTRODUCTION OF ISLAM, ARABS CAPTURED IRAQ FROM THE SASANIANS. SOON, IRAQ BECAME AN ISLAMIC, MOSTLY ARAB, REGION WHICH IT REMAINS TO THIS DAY.[26]

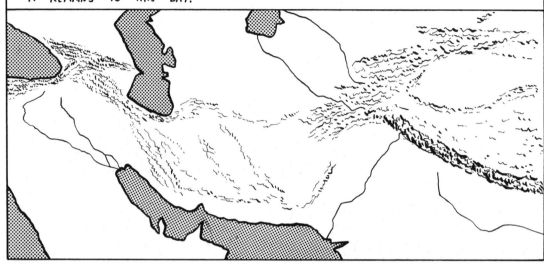

THE TERM AL IRAQ IS ARABIC FOR "THE SHORE OF A BIG RIVER AND THE LAND SURROUNDING IT." IN 762, BAGHDAD WAS BUILT, AND WAS THE CAPITAL OF THE ABBASID CALIPHATE.[27, 28]

THE CITY WAS SACKED IN 1258 BY MONGOLS UNDER HULAGU KHAN, GRANDSON OF GENGHIS KHAN OR CHINGGIS KHAN. THE INVASION RESULTED IN THE MASSACRE OF THOUSANDS.

EVENTUALLY, THE LEADERSHIP OF THE ISLAMIC WORLD PASSED TO THE OTTOMANS IN 1453. THEY RULED MUCH OF THE MIDDLE EAST, INCLUDING IRAQ. TURIC PEOPLE FROM CENTRAL ASIA, THE OTTOMANS HAD ONE OF THE GREATEST EMPIRES IN HISTORY. SULEIMAN THE MAGNIFICENT WAS THE RULER WHEN IRAQ WAS CONQUERED.

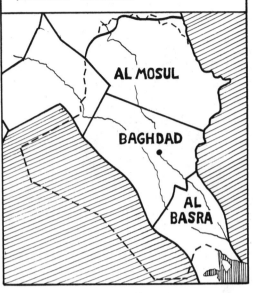

IRAQ WAS RULED AS THREE SEPARATE PROVINCES BASED ON ETHNIC AND RELIGIOUS DIVISIONS.

AL MOSUL

BAGHDAD

AL BASRA

SO WAIT, WAIT, WHAT IS A SHIA? OR IS IT A SHIITE?

WAR

I MUST HAVE BEEN ASKED A HUNDRED TIMES TO EXPLAIN THE RELIGIOUS SECTS AND ETHNIC GROUPS OF IRAQ.

I GUESS IT DOESN'T REALLY MATTER IN ENGLISH.

OK BUT HOW DOES THAT WORK? ARE THEY ARABS OR IRAQIS?

THEY ARE BOTH... LISTEN, MOST IRAQIS ARE ARABS, WHICH IS AN ETHNICITY LIKE GERMAN OR WHATEVER...

OK, SO WHAT'S A SHIITE?

IT'S A BRANCH OF ISLAM, THEY ARE THE MAJORITY IN IRAQ, LIKE 60 PERCENT, SUNNI ARABS ARE 20 PERCENT.

AMERICA'S FIRST "WAR ON TERROR" GOES BACK TO THE TIME THE OTTOMANS RULED. THE FIRST TWO LINES OF THE U.S. MARINES' "BATTLE HYMN" ARE: "FROM THE HALLS OF MONTEZUMA TO THE SHORES OF TRIPOLI."

THE FIRST PART REFERS TO THE MEXICAN-AMERICAN WAR.

THE SECOND PART REFERS TO AMERICA'S INVOLVEMENT IN THE BARBARY WAR 1801-1805. IT BEGAN WHEN PIRATES OF NORTH AFRICAN STATES SEIZED AMERICAN SHIPS & DEMANDED PAYMENT FOR SAFE PASSAGE OFF OF THE NORTH AFRICAN COAST.[29]

THOMAS JEFFERSON REFUSED TO PAY, AND THIS RESULTED IN WAR.

THE MARINES AND U.S. NAVY BECAME A FIXTURE IN THE MILITARY.[30]

THERE ARE ABOUT 25 MILLION KURDS LIVING MOSTLY IN THE MIDDLE EAST. THEY ARE DISPERSED THROUGHOUT THE REGION WITH POPULATIONS IN IRAQ, SYRIA, IRAN, AND TURKEY. KURDS ARE THE LARGEST NATION IN THE WORLD WITHOUT A STATE, BUT AFTER THE 1991 GULF WAR THEY ESTABLISHED A SEMI-AUTONOMOUS ZONE IN NORTHERN IRAQ. THE MAJORITY (15 MILLION) LIVE IN TURKEY.

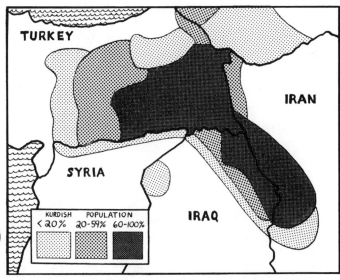

AFTER WORLD WAR I, THE OTTOMAN EMPIRE COLLAPSED AND THE MIDDLE EAST WAS DIVIDED BETWEEN THE EUROPEAN ALLIES: FRANCE AND BRITAIN.

THE EUROPEAN POWERS CHOSE TO DENY THE KURDS A STATE WHEN THEY RE-DREW THE BORDERS OF THE MIDDLE EAST IN 1916 WITH THE SYKES-PICOT AGREEMENT.

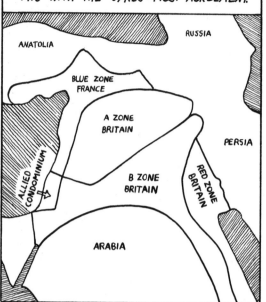

IT'S IRONIC THAT IN THE LEAD UP TO THE 2003 INVASION AMERICAN LEADERS CITED THE SUFFERING OF THE KURDS UNDER SADDAM HUSSEIN.

HE GASSED HIS OWN PEOPLE!

IN THE 1990s, THE TURKISH GOVERNMENT WENT ON A BLOODY CAMPAIGN OF ETHNIC CLEANSING AGAINST REBELLING KURDS IN EASTERN TURKEY. ENTIRE VILLAGES WERE DEVASTATED AS THE TURKISH MILITARY RAMPAGED THROUGH THE COUNTRYSIDE.

THE CLINTON ADMINISTRATION ARMED THE TURKISH MILITARY AT THE HEIGHT OF THE KILLING TO THE TUNE OF BILLIONS OF DOLLARS.[31]

IN 1901, A VERY SAVVY BRITISH ENTREPRENEUR, WILLIAM KNOX D'ARCY, WAS GRANTED THE FIRST OIL CONCESSION IN THE MIDDLE EAST FROM THE IRANIAN MONARCHY.

THE EXTREMELY FAVORABLE TERMS OF THE DEAL GAVE D'ARCY THE "EXCLUSIVE PRIVILEGE" TO EXPLOIT OIL "THROUGHOUT THE WHOLE EXTENT OF THE PERSIAN EMPIRE FOR A TERM OF 60 YEARS." THE GOVERNMENT WOULD GET 16% OF NET PROFITS.[32]

FROM 1914 TO 1921 BRITAIN MILITARILY OCCUPIED IRAQ AND DREW THE BORDERS THAT EXIST TO THIS DAY. THIS MODERN IRAQ WAS LANDLOCKED, LOSING ITS SOUTHERN PROVINCE THAT BECAME KUWAIT — THIS OF COURSE, WOULD HAVE IMPLICATIONS LATER.

LIKE MOST MILITARY OCCUPATIONS, THE BRITISH ONE WAS BRUTAL, AND WAS VIOLENTLY OPPOSED BY IRAQIS. IN 1920, A REVOLT BROKE OUT, AND WAS RUTHLESSLY PUT DOWN BY THE BRITISH, RESULTING IN THOUSANDS OF DEATHS. THE BRITISH EVEN USED MUSTARD GAS ON THE REBELS, DROPPING IT FROM PLANES.[33]

WHEN BRITAIN WAS CHALLENGED OVER THE USE OF AERIAL BOMBARDMENT OF CIVILIANS, STATESMAN LLOYD GEORGE SAID:

WE INSISTED ON RESERVING THE RIGHT TO BOMB NIGGERS.[34]

THE GREAT WINSTON CHURCHILL ALSO GAVE HIS HONEST OPINION OF ARABS WHEN HE SAID:

THE ARABS ARE A BACKWARDS PEOPLE WHO EAT NOTHING BUT CAMEL DUNG.[35]

IT WAS A YOUNG CHURCHILL WHO, IN HIS CAPACITY AS THE FIRST LORD OF THE ADMIRALTY, MADE THE DECISION TO CONVERT THE BRITISH FLEET FROM COAL POWER TO OIL IN 1911. IN 1912, HE SIGNED AN AGREEMENT WITH THE ANGLO-PERSIAN OIL COMPANY, WHICH HAD WELLS NEAR BASRA. IT BECAME MORE ESSENTIAL THAN EVER TO BE IN THAT VITAL AREA.

LATER, AS COLONIAL SECRETARY, CHURCHILL PRESIDED OVER THE CAIRO CONFERENCE OF 1921 WHERE IT WAS DECIDED THAT IRAQ SHOULD BECOME A KINGDOM UNDER-BRITISH TUTELAGE OF COURSE.

THE FAMED GERTRUDE BELL WAS IN ATTENDACE - ITS BEEN SAID THAT SHE LITERALLY DREW THE BORDERS OF IRAQ ON A BLANK MAP.

ALSO PRESENT WAS T.E. LAWRENCE, BETTER KNOWN AS "LAWRENCE OF ARABIA", OF THE ARAB REVOLT DURING WORLD WAR I.

IN 1921 AMIR FAISAL, THE NON-IRAQI LEADER OF THE ARAB REVOLT, WAS CHOSEN BY THE BRITISH TO BE KING, (AN "ARAB FACADE" TO BRITISH CONTROL) AND WAS ENTHRONED LATER THAT YEAR TO THE TUNE OF "GOD SAVE THE KING." [36]

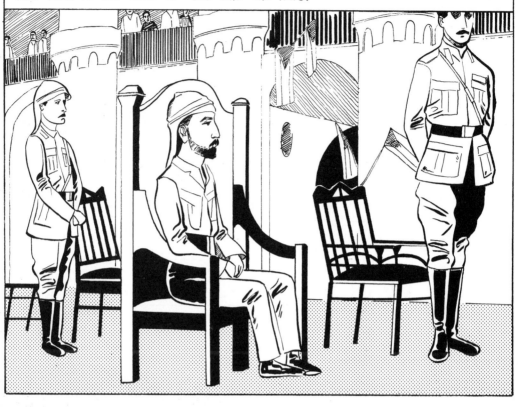

IRAQ WAS GIVEN FORMAL INDEPENDENCE IN 1932, BUT OF COURSE KING FAISAL AND HIS REGIME WERE STILL SUBSERVIENT TO THE BRITISH.

WHILE THE FRENCH AND BRITISH WERE SEEN AS AGGRESIVE IMPERIAL POWERS IN THE MIDDLE EAST, THE U.S. WAS VIEWED MORE POSITIVELY. PRESIDENT WILSON'S "14 POINTS," ANNUNCIATED DURING WWI, WAS SEEN AS PROMOTING SELF-DETERMINATION.

SAUDI ARABIA, FOUNDED IN 1927, WAS ONE OF THE FEW COUNTRIES OF THE MIDDLE EAST THAT WAS REALLY INDEPENDENT. IN 1933 THE SAUDI GOVERNMENT SIGNED AN OIL DEAL WITH STANDARD OIL OF CALIFORNIA, WHICH LATER BECAME THE ARABIAN AMERICAN OIL COMPANY: ARAMCO. OIL WAS DISCOVERED IN 1938. ROOSEVELT MET WITH KING SAUD IN 1944.

THE RELATIONSHIP BETWEEN THE U.S. AND SAUDI ARABIA, THE WORLD'S LARGEST SOURCE OF OIL, HAS BEEN STRONG EVER SINCE.

WORLD WAR II RESULTED IN THE END OF THE BRITISH EMPIRE AND THE EMERGENCE OF THE U.S. AS THE MAJOR POWER IN THE MIDDLE EAST. WITH THE START OF THE COLD WAR, THE U.S. SAW THE MIDDLE EAST AS A BATTLEGROUND AGAINST SOVIET INFLUENCE, AND A REGION THAT NEEDED TO STAY UNDER U.S. DOMINATION.

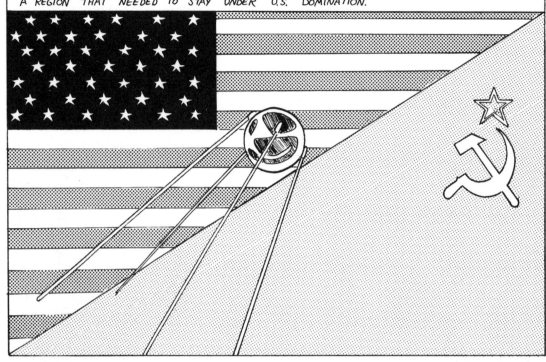

BUT SOVIET INFLUENCE WAS MOSTLY A PRETEXT FOR THE U.S. CONTROLLING WHAT PRESIDENT EISENHOWER CALLED:

THE MOST STRATEGICALLY IMPORTANT AREA IN THE WORLD.

INDIGENOUS NATIONALISM, HOWEVER, WAS A MORE SERIOUS THREAT TO U.S. INTERESTS, MORE ON THAT LATER...

IN 1948 ISRAEL WAS CREATED AFTER 700,000 [37] PALESTINIANS WERE REMOVED OR FLED THE FIGHTING, AND AMERICA, UNDER PRESIDENT TRUMAN, WAS THE FIRST COUNTRY TO RECOGNIZE THE NEW ZIONIST STATE.

WHILE THE PALESTINIANS BECAME REFUGEES WHO STILL HAVE NO STATE OF THEIR OWN. THESE EVENTS WOULD HAVE REPERCUSSIONS TO THIS DAY.

IN 1946, GEORGE KENNAN INTRODUCED THE "CONTAINMENT POLICY," WHICH BECAME THE "TRUMAN DOCTRINE," WHICH SOUGHT TO COMBAT COMMUNISM IN ANY PART OF THE WORLD WITH THE USE OF ECONOMIC/MILITARY AID — EVEN OUTRIGHT INTERVENTION.

THE FIRST APPLICATION OF THE DOCTRINE WAS IN GREECE WHERE AN INSURGENCY WAS PUT DOWN VIOLENTLY.

THERE SEEMED TO BE A TACIT UNDERSTANDING THAT THE MEDITERRANEAN, AND THE MIDDLE EAST, WERE TO BE PART OF THE AMERICAN "ZONE OF INFLUENCE." IN OTHER WORDS, THE MONROE DOCTRINE WAS EXTENDED TO INCLUDE THE MIDDLE EAST.

GREECE

AEGEAN SEA

TURKEY

ATHENS

MEDITERRANEAN SEA

THE MIDDLE EAST'S OIL IS THE PRINCIPAL REASON FOR WESTERN INVOLVEMENT. NOAM CHOMSKY SAID:

IF IRAQ'S MAIN EXPORT WERE LETTUCE, WE WOULDN'T BE TALKING ABOUT ANY OF THIS.

THESE WARS ARE OVER OIL MAN! THAT'S WHAT THIS WHOLE THING IS ABOUT!

WELL I THINK THAT'S PARTLY TRUE.

LOOK, THAT'S WHAT IT'S ALL ABOUT, PROFITS, OIL, THAT'S IT.

WELL YES, BUT...

WHAT IS MOST IMPORTANT TO THE WEST (AND INCREASINGLY, THE EAST) IS NOT SO MUCH PROFITS, BUT ACCESS...

IN THE 1940s, A STATE DEPARTMENT OFFICIAL SAID SAUDI RESERVES:

CONSTITUTE A STUPENDOUS SOURCE OF STRATEGIC POWER, AND ONE OF THE GREATEST PRIZES IN WORLD HISTORY.[38]

AS THE U.S. BECAME THE POWER IN THE REGION, IT TIGHTENED CONTROL.

AND WITH ITS DOMINATION OF THE WESTERN HEMISPHERE, PLUS THE FACT THE U.S. WAS ACTUALLY A NET EXPORTER OF OIL UNTIL 1968,[39] UNCLE SAM WAS STRATEGICALLY WELL POSITIONED.

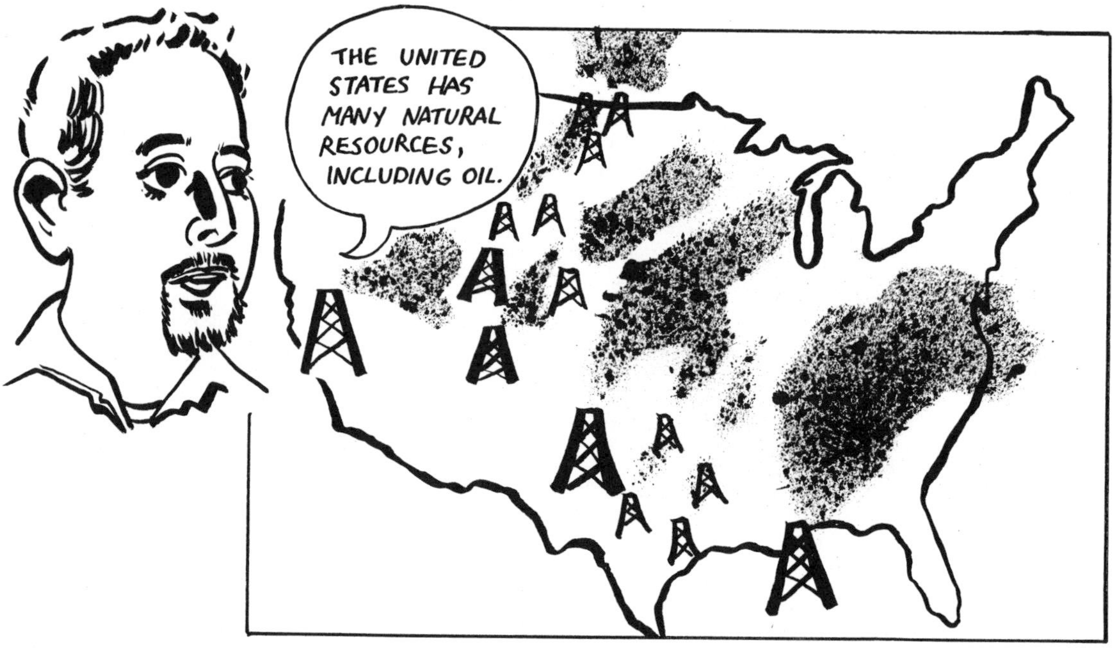
THE UNITED STATES HAS MANY NATURAL RESOURCES, INCLUDING OIL.

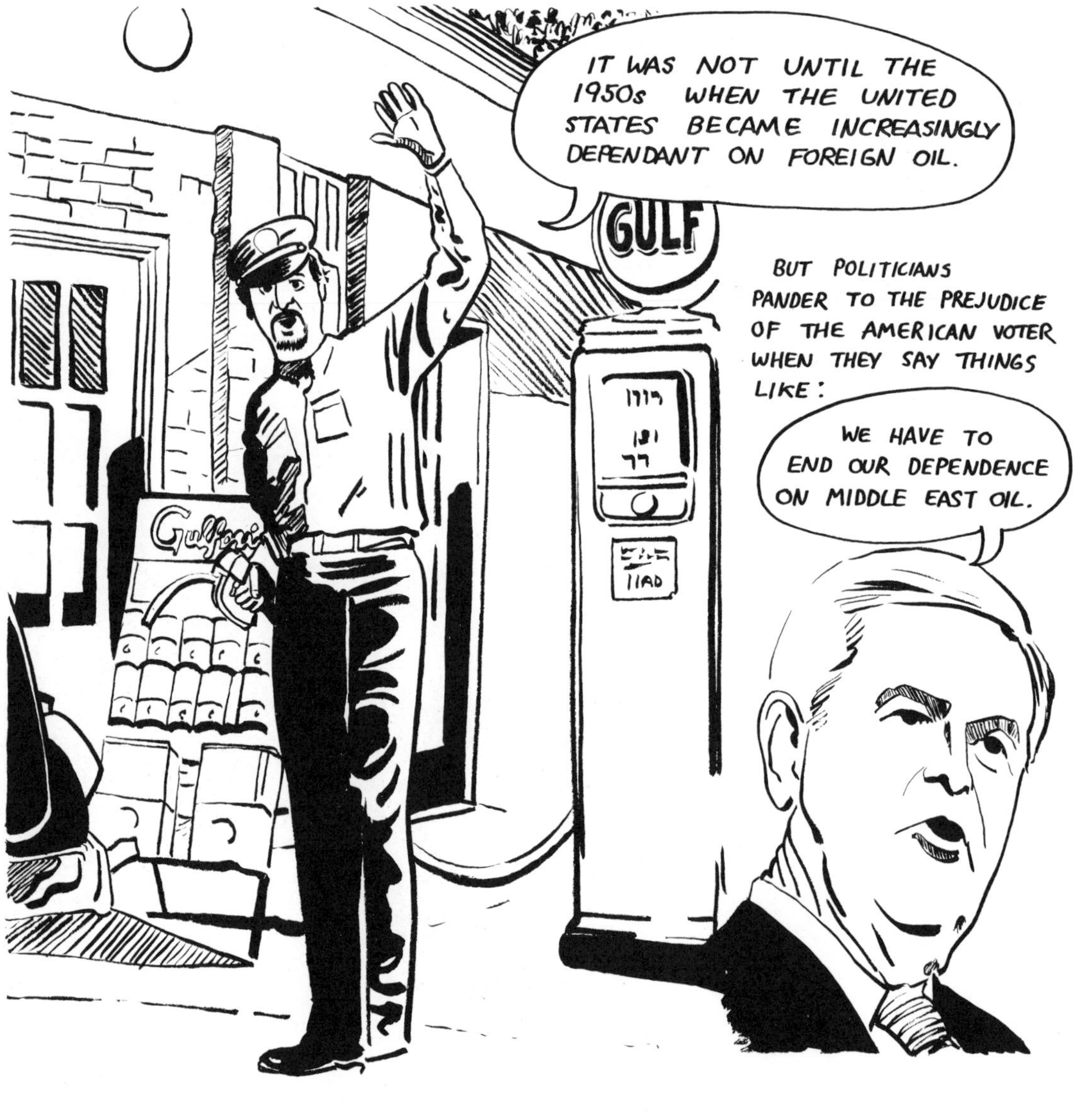
IT WAS NOT UNTIL THE 1950s WHEN THE UNITED STATES BECAME INCREASINGLY DEPENDANT ON FOREIGN OIL.
GULF
BUT POLITICIANS PANDER TO THE PREJUDICE OF THE AMERICAN VOTER WHEN THEY SAY THINGS LIKE:
WE HAVE TO END OUR DEPENDENCE ON MIDDLE EAST OIL.

IN THE LAST FEW YEARS, US OIL PRODUCTION HAS RISEN SO MUCH THAT IT MAY OVERTAKE THE MIDDLE EAST'S OUTPUT.[40]

IN 2012, THE U.S. WAS PRODUCING 10.9 MILLION BARRELS A DAY COMPARED TO SAUDI ARABIA'S 11.6 MILLION, THE BIGGEST INCREASE SINCE 1951.[41]

OIL EXPERT JIM BURKHARD SAID:

FIVE YEARS AGO, IF I OR ANYONE PREDICTED TODAY'S PRODUCTION GROWTH, PEOPLE WOULD HAVE SAID WE WERE CRAZY.

CITIBANK PREDICTS THAT THE U.S. COULD BE PRODUCING UP TO 15 MILLION BARRELS BY 2020.[42]

HOWEVER, THE UNITED STATES WILL STILL HAVE TO IMPORT OIL BECAUSE AMERICANS USE ABOUT 19 MILLION BARRELS A DAY— THE MOST IN THE WORLD.[43]

AS TRADITIONAL SOURCES OF OIL BECOME INACCESSIBLE, SQUEEZING OIL OUT OF ROCK & SHALE (KNOWN AS "FRACKING") IS ONE WAY PRODUCTION HAS INCREASED.

BY PUMPING WATER, SAND, AND CHEMICALS INTO THE ROCK, DRILLERS ARE ABLE TO RELEASE THE OIL. BESIDES ENVIRONMENTAL ISSUES, THE PROCCESS CAN CONTAMINATE DRINKING WATER WITH FLAMMABLE AND POISONOUS CHEMICALS.

IN 2011, U.S. CRUDE IMPORTS FELL TO THE LOWEST LEVEL IN YEARS. IMPORTS COME MAINLY FROM 5 COUNTRIES: MEXICO, WHICH IS DEALING WITH AN EXTREMLY BLOODY DRUG WAR...

VENEZUELA, WHICH HAS BEEN HOSTILE TO THE UNITED STATES LATELY...

AND RECENTLY, NIGERIA WHICH HAS BEEN SUFFERING CIVIL UNREST DISRUPTING THE FLOW OF OIL. DUTCH SHELL HAS BEEN ACCUSED OF FUNDING MILITANTS IN THE NIGER DELTA, FUELING A CONFLICT THAT COSTS THOUSANDS OF LIVES A YEAR.[44]

CANADA IS THE ONLY STABLE SOURCE.

OIL IS A FINITE RESOURCE. IN FACT, MANY HAVE BEEN PREDICTING "PEAK OIL" FOR DECADES.[45]

THE CHEAP PRICE OF GAS IN THE U.S. HAS CREATED AN AUTOMOBILE-CENTERED SOCIETY GOING BACK TO AT LEAST THE 1950s.

WHENEVER GAS PRICES DIP, THE DISCUSSION ABOUT CLIMATE CHANGE IS PUT OFF.

HENRY FORD WOULD LIKELY BE SURPRISED THAT WE STILL USE INTERNAL COMBUSTION ENGINES.

THE MOST CURRENT ESTIMATES ARE THAT OIL WILL PEEK BETWEEN NOW & 2040.[46]

THERE ARE OVER ONE TRILLION BARRELS OF OIL IN THE WORLD.[47]

NOT TOO LONG AGO, OIL WAS GOING FOR ABOUT 100 DOLLARS A BARREL.

THOUGH PRICES FLUCTUATE, THE WORLD'S DEPENDENCE ON OIL IS CONSTANT.

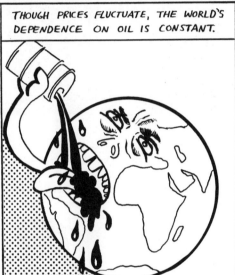

AT 100 DOLLARS A BARREL, I THINK PROFITS WILL OUTWEIGH ANY CONCERN FOR THE ENVIRONMENT FOR NOW.

MULTINATIONAL OIL COMPANIES HAVE ENORMOUS INFLUENCE OVER GOVERNMENTS, & THAT'S NOT LIKELY TO CHANGE SOON.

IN FACT, OIL COMPANIES ARE THE MOST PROFITABLE CORPORATIONS IN THE WORLD. IN 2012, EXXON MOBILE MADE 15.9 BILLION IN JUST ONE QUARTER.[48]

THAT SET A WORLD RECORD.

BY 1953, THE BRITISH HAD SIGNIFICANT
CONTROL OVER PERSIAN GULF OIL.
IN FACT, THE BRITISH GOVERNMENT
OWNED MORE THAN 50% OF THE
ANGLO-PERSIAN OIL COMPANY.[49]
NEEDLESS TO SAY, IRANIANS
CHAFFED AT THIS UNFAIR SITUATION,
AND IN THE SAME YEAR MOHAMMAD
MOSADDEQ, A SECULAR NATIONALIST,
WAS DEMOCRATICALLY ELECTED
IRAN'S PRIME MINISTER.

HE MOVED TO NATIONALIZE IRAN'S
OIL INDUSTRY. THIS ATTEMPT
PROMPTED THE BRITISH TO SEEK
HIS OUSTER. AND SO THE BRITISH
MI6 COLLUDED WITH THE CIA
TO OVERTHOW MOSADDEQ, AND
REPLACE HIM WITH A LESS
THREATENING LEADER.[50] THIS WAS
THE FIRST OF MANY OVERTHROWS
THE CIA WOULD BE RESPONSIBLE
FOR DURING THE COLD WAR.

KERMIT ROOSEVELT, SON OF TEDDY
ROOSEVELT, WAS A CIA AGENT WHO PLAYED
A KEY ROLE IN THE OVERTHROW. HE
DETAILS HIS EXPLOITS IN HIS (HARD TO
FIND) BOOK "COUNTER COUP."

SHAH MUHAMMAD REZA PAHLAVI, "THE KING
OF KINGS," WAS INSTALLED AND RULED
THE COUNTRY WITH AN IRON FIST-WITH THE
SUPPORT OF THE UNITED STATES.

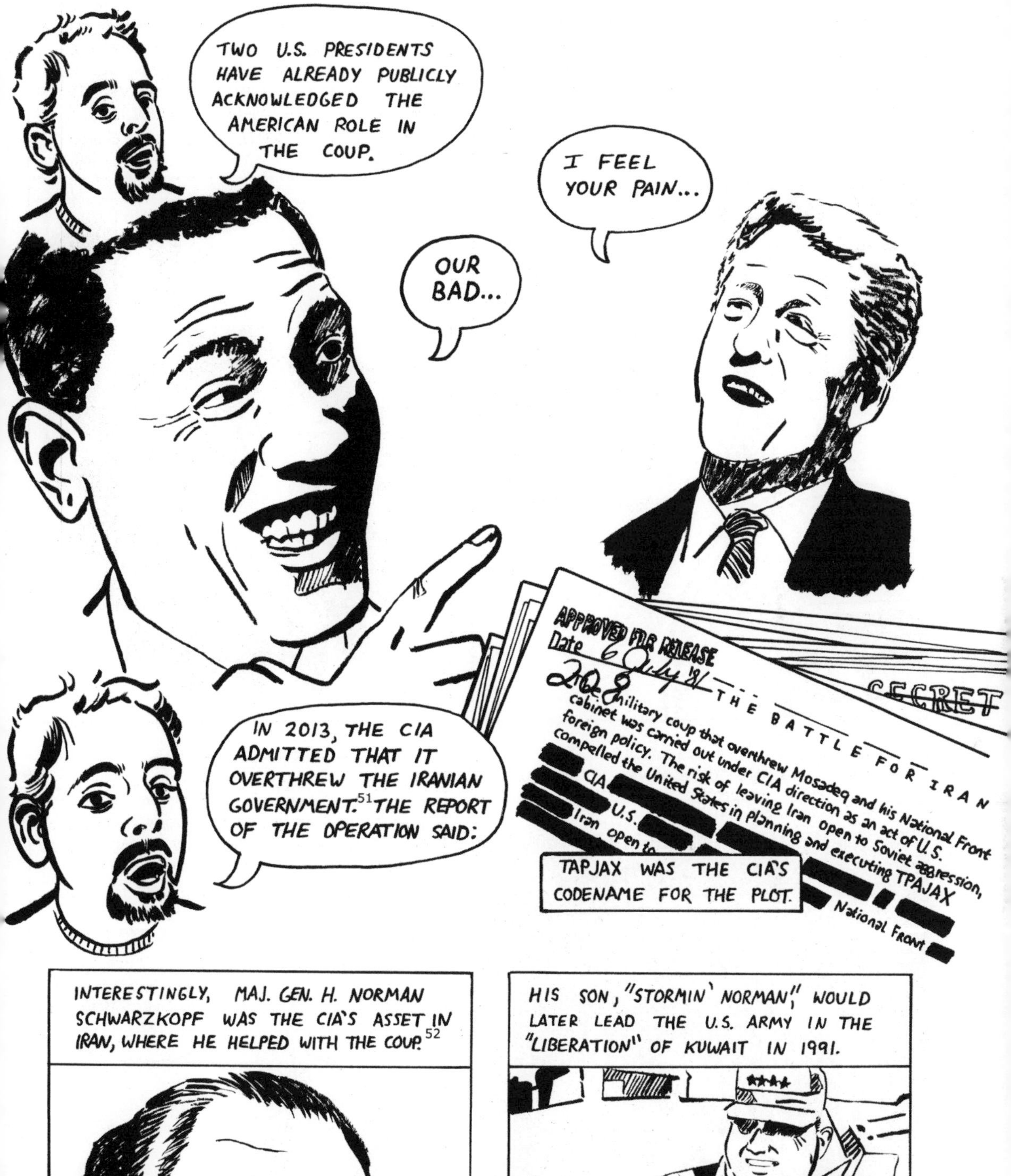
TWO U.S. PRESIDENTS HAVE ALREADY PUBLICLY ACKNOWLEDGED THE AMERICAN ROLE IN THE COUP.
OUR BAD...
I FEEL YOUR PAIN...
IN 2013, THE CIA ADMITTED THAT IT OVERTHREW THE IRANIAN GOVERNMENT.[51] THE REPORT OF THE OPERATION SAID:
APPROVED FOR RELEASE
Date 6 July '81
SECRET
THE BATTLE FOR IRAN
The military coup that overthrew Mosadeq and his National Front cabinet was carried out under CIA direction as an act of U.S. foreign policy. The risk of leaving Iran open to Soviet aggression, compelled the United States in planning and executing TPAJAX
[redacted] CIA [redacted] U.S. [redacted] Iran open to [redacted] National Front [redacted]
TAPJAX WAS THE CIA'S CODENAME FOR THE PLOT.
INTERESTINGLY, MAJ. GEN. H. NORMAN SCHWARZKOPF WAS THE CIA'S ASSET IN IRAN, WHERE HE HELPED WITH THE COUP.[52]
HIS SON, "STORMIN' NORMAN," WOULD LATER LEAD THE U.S. ARMY IN THE "LIBERATION" OF KUWAIT IN 1991.

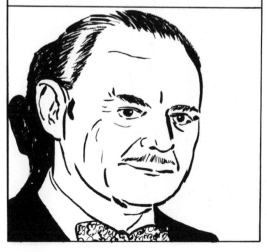

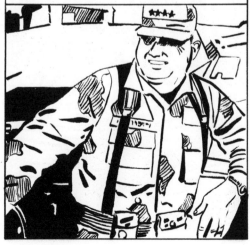

THE SHAH RESTORED ANGLO-PERSIAN OIL COMPANY'S POSITION IN IRAN BUT, AS A REWARD FOR AMERICAN PARTICIPATION IN THE COUP, 40 PERCENT OF IRAN'S OIL WENT TO U.S. OIL COMPANIES.[53]

ANGLO-PERSIAN OIL EVENTUALLY BECAME BRITISH PETROLEUM OR BP WHICH, AS OF 2010, IS THE 10TH LARGEST CORPORATION IN THE WORLD WITH YEARLY REVENUE AT 226 BILLION IN 2016,[54] AND 25 BILLION IN PROFITS.[55]

IN APRIL 2010, BP'S DRILLING IN THE GULF OF MEXICO CAUSED THE WORST ENVIRONMENTAL DISASTER IN U.S. HISTORY.

THE SHAH'S POWER ESSENTIALLY RESTED ON THE CRUCIAL BACKING OF THE UNITED STATES. SUPPRESSION OF POLITICAL PARTIES (ESPECIALLY OF THE COMMUNIST TUDEH PARTY) WAS COMMON. KHOSROW ROOZBEH, A LEADER OF THE TUDEH, WAS EXECUTED IN 1958 AND IS STILL CONSIDERED A MARTYR BY MANY.[56]

LONG LIVE THE TUDEH PARTY OF IRAN! LONG LIVE COMMUNISM! FIRE![57]

IN 1957, WITH THE CIA'S HELP, IRAN CREATED THE DREADED SECRET POLICE KNOWN AS THE SAVAK,[58] WHICH TORTURED AND KILLED THOUSANDS OF DISSIDENTS AND ORDINARY PEOPLE DURING THE SHAH'S RULE.[59]

IN 1976, AMNESTY INTERNATIONAL ESTIMATED THAT 25,000 TO 100,000 PEOPLE WERE BEING HELD AS "PRISONERS OF CONSCIENCE" IN IRAN. ELECTRIC SHOCK, BURNING ON A HEATED METAL GRILL, AND INSERTION OF BOTTLES AND HOT EGGS INTO THE ANUS, WERE ALL METHODS USED BY THE SECRET POLICE. MANY WERE TORTURED TO DEATH, INCLUDING A NUMBER OF WOMEN WHO WERE MUTILATED.[60]

REZA BARAHENI, AN IRANIAN POET, WAS PRISONER FOR 102 DAYS IN 1973 AND RELEASED ONLY AFTER HE MADE A TELEVISED STATEMENT CONDEMNING COMMUNISM.

"THEY HANG YOU UPSIDE DOWN, AND THEN SOMEONE BEATS YOU WITH A MACE ON YOUR LEGS OR ON YOUR GENITALS, OR THEY LOWER YOU DOWN, PULL YOUR PANTS UP AND THEN ONE OF THEM TRIES TO RAPE YOU WHILE YOU ARE STILL HANGING UPSIDE DOWN."[61]

THE SHAH EXPORTED 7% OF THE NON-COMMUNIST WORLD'S OIL AND REFUSED TO JOIN THE 1973 ARAB OIL EMBARGO. HIS REGIME WAS MARKED BY CORRUPTION, AND HIS FORCED WESTERNIZATION POLICIES, WERE DEEPLY UNPOPULAR.[62]

WHEN IRANIANS LEARN TO BEHAVE LIKE SWEDES, I WILL BEHAVE LIKE THE KING OF SWEDEN.[63]

MANY AMERICANS ASSOCIATE IRAN WITH TERRORISM AND ISLAMIC RADICALISM. FEW KNOW THAT IT WAS A MAJOR U.S. ALLY.

IRANIANS ARE NOT ARABS...

WHAT? THAN WHAT ARE THEY?

THEY ARE IRANIAN.

?...

IRANIANS ARE INDO-EUROPEAN. THEIR LANGUAGE ISN'T SEMETIC LIKE ARABIC OR HEBREW.

PERSIA BECAME IRAN IN 1935 WHEN IT CHANGED ITS NAME TO EMPHASIZE ITS "ARYAN" ROOTS. IRAN MEANS "LAND OF THE ARYANS." [64]

BUT THEY AREN'T WHITE.

THE TWO PILLARS OF U.S. POWER IN THE MIDDLE EAST WERE ISRAEL AND IRAN. NIXON ONCE CALLED ISRAEL:

OUR COP ON THE BEAT.

ACCORDING TO A SENATE COMMITTEE REPORT, "THREATS TO THE CONTINUOUS FLOW OF OIL THROUGH THE GULF WOULD BE GROUNDS FOR GENERAL WAR." AND A "STRONG STABLE IRAN" SERVES AS A DETERRENT AGAINST RADICAL GROUPS IN THE GULF.[65]

SENATE COMMITTEE

UNITED STATES
SENATE

TURKEY

SYRIA

JORDAN

IRAQ

IRAN

EGYPT

A YEAR BEFORE THE SHAH TOOK POWER IN IRAN, EGYPT (THE MOST POPULOUS ARAB COUNTRY) EXPERIENCED A MILITARY COUP, WHICH OUSTED THE PLAYBOY KING FAROUK.

THE "FREE OFFICERS" WERE NATIONALISTS AND PART OF THE IDEOLOGICAL MILIEU OF THE PERIOD WHEN SECULAR IDEOLOGIES PREVAILED.

GAMAL ABDEL NASSER BECAME THE CHARISMATIC LEADER OF EGYPT, AND POPULARIZED ARAB NATIONALISM, AND THE IDEA OF PAN-ARABISM.

NASSER WAS NOT A COMMUNIST, BUT HE WAS A NATIONALIST. THE MYTH OF THE SPREADING COMMUNIST MENACE IS CONTRADICTED BY THE WEST'S RESPONSE TO NASSER.

INITIALLY, HE HAD NO INTEREST IN ALLYING WITH EITHER THE U.S. OR U.S.S.R. HE HELPED FORM THE NON-ALIGNED MOVEMENT WITH:

JAWAHARLAL NEHRU OF INDIA

KWAME NKRUMAH OF GHANA

SUKARNO OF INDONESIA

JOSIP BROZ TITO OF YUGOSLAVIA

THE CONCEPT OF NEUTRALITY IN THE COLD WAR DID NOT SIT WELL WITH SECRETARY OF STATE JOHN FOSTER DULLES.

NEUTRALITY IS SUICIDE.

49

TAKING THEIR CUE FROM EGYPT, "THE FOUR COLONELS" OF IRAQ OVERTHREW KING FAISAL II IN 1958.

THE PRO-WESTERN KING WAS KILLED IN THE RESULTING VIOLENCE AGAINST THE HATED MONARCHY.

THE LEADER, BRIGADIER GENERAL QASIM, WAS AN ARAB NATIONALIST, AND WAS PART OF THE TIDE IN THE MIDDLE EAST THAT THREATENED THE TRADITIONAL REGIMES THAT WERE SUBORDINATE TO WESTERN POWER.

SOON, QASIM BEGAN TO ASSERT IRAQ'S INDEPENDENCE, AND WAS SEEN AS A THREAT TO U.S. INTERESTS. THE CIA, UNDER PRESIDENT KENNEDY, MOVED TO REMOVE QASIM FROM POWER.[66]

IN A FAILED ATTEMPT TO ASSASINATE HIM, THE CIA'S "HEALTH ALTERATION COMMITTEE," SENT QASIM A MONOGRAMMED, POISONED HANDKERCHIEF.[67]

THIS WAS IN KEEPING WITH THE MANY ABSURD CIA ATTEMPTS AT KILLING FIDEL CASTRO AND DESTABILIZING THE CUBAN GOVERNMENT. IT WAS DUBBED "OPERATION MONGOOSE."

Qasim

BAM

ONE PLOT INCLUDED AN EXPLODING CIGAR![68]

ANOTHER PLOT WAS TO POISON CASTRO SO HIS BEARD WOULD FALL OUT![69]

RAL INTELLIG

WHILE THE COLD WAR, AND QASIM'S TOLERANCE OF COMMUNISTS, WERE DECLARED MOTIVATIONS OF THE U.S. - IT IS ALSO IMPORTANT TO NOTE THAT THE U.S. WAS ACTING IN ACCORDANCE WITH ITS INTERESTS. BOTH FEAR OF COMMUNISM, AND CONCERN ABOUT MIDDLE EASTERN INDEPENDENCE FROM THE WEST, COMPELLED THE U.S. & ITS ALLIES.

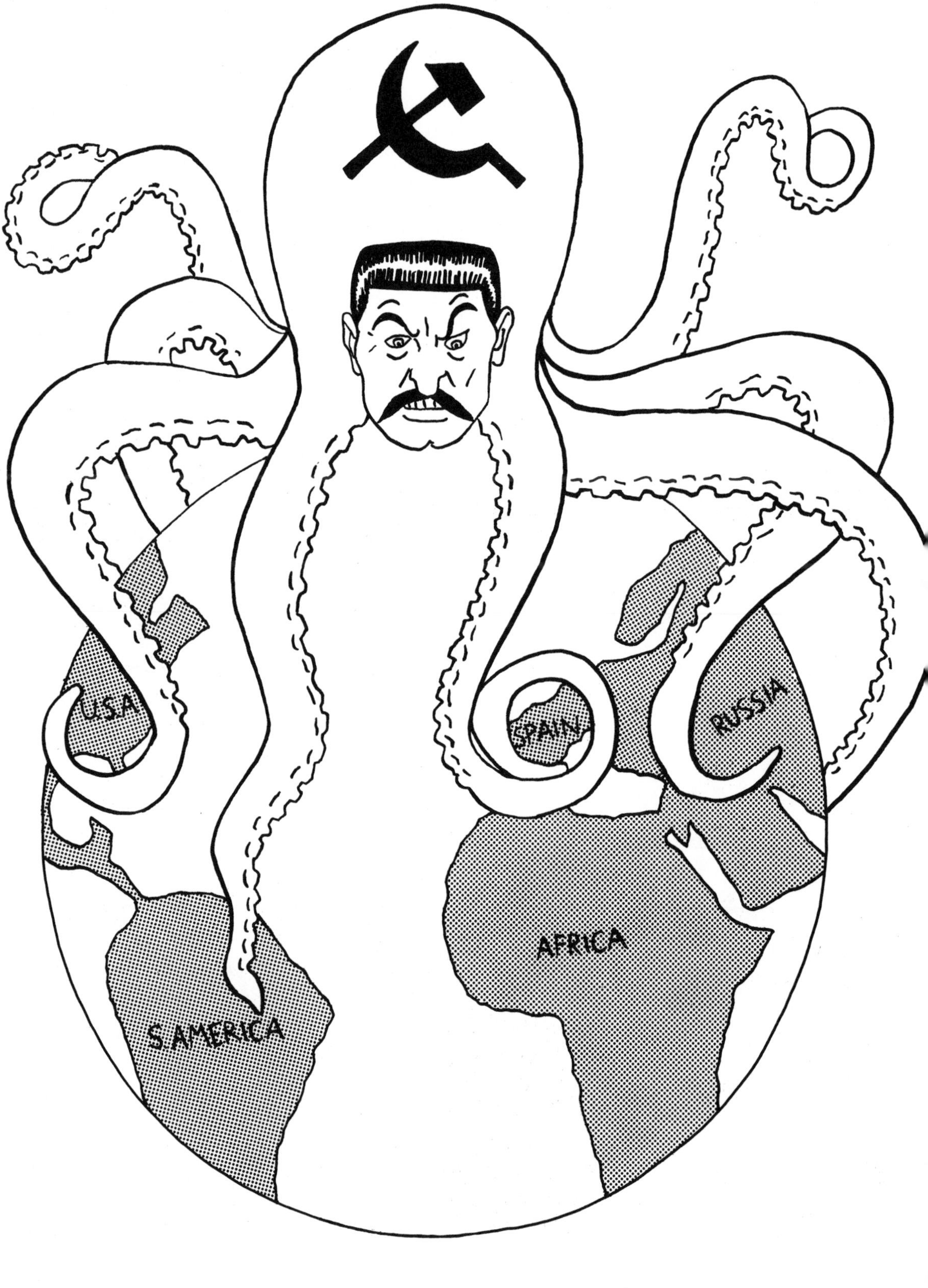
USA
SPAIN
RUSSIA
AFRICA
S.AMERICA

IN 1956 THE U.S. BACKED OUT OF AN AGREEMENT TO HELP EGYPT BUILD THE ASWAN DAM ON THE NILE. PRESIDENT NASSER RESPONDED BY NATIONALIZING THE SUEZ CANAL IN ORDER TO PAY FOR THE DAM WITH THE TOLL MONEY.

THAT YEAR, A BRITISH, FRENCH, AND ISRAELI ALLIANCE SOUGHT TO RESTORE EUROPEAN CONTROL WHEN THEY INVADED EGYPT.

THIS WAS THE LAST GASP OF EUROPEAN EMPIRE IN THE MIDDLE EAST. NOW A COLD WAR ARENA, THE UNITED STATES FORCED THE EUROPEANS & ISRAELIS TO WITHDRAW. IT WAS ALSO THE END OF ANTHONY EDEN'S CAREER AS THE PRIME MINISTER OF BRITAIN.

SOME COMPARE HIS MISCALCULATION TO TONY BLAIR'S DECISION TO JOIN THE U.S. IN THE INVASION OF IRAQ.

THE SOVIETS BACKED EGYPT, AND NIKITA KHRUSHCHEV THREATENED TO BOMB ENGLAND AND FRANCE.

ALL THIS WAS HAPPENING WHILE A REVOLT BROKE OUT IN SOVIET CONTROLLED HUNGARY AFTER KHRUSHCHEV DENOUNCED STALIN. NUCLEAR WAR WAS FEARED.

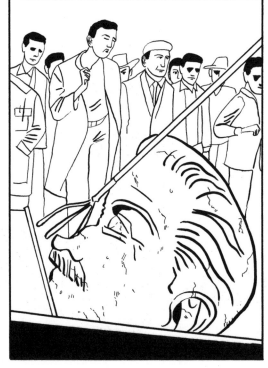

NASSER BECAME A HERO OF THE ARAB WORLD, AND HIS BRAND OF NATIONALISM, OR NASSERISM GAINED INFLUENCE. THE CRISIS ALSO STRENGTHENED EGYPTIAN/SOVIET TIES, WHICH FURTHERED THE IRE OF THE UNITED STATES.

ALSO, IN RESPONSE TO THE CRISIS, THE EISENHOWER DOCTRINE WAS BORN — IN WHICH THE UNITED STATES PROVIDED MILITARY ASSISTANCE TO ANY MIDDLE EASTERN COUNTRY DEEMED TO BE "RESISTING COMMUNISM."

THIS REMINDED NASSER OF THE BAGHDAD PACT OF 1955, AN ANTI-COMMUNIST ALLIANCE CREATED UNDER THE GUIDANCE OF THE UNITED STATES.

MEMBERS OF THE PACT INCLUDED PAKISTAN, IRAN, TURKEY, THE UK, AND IRAQ. IN 1959 QASIM TOOK IRAQ OUT OF THE BAGHDAD PACT. THEY EVEN HAD A COOL FLAG.

IN THE EARLY 50s, IRAQ NEGOTIATED A NEW CONTRACT WITH EUROPEAN OWNED IRAQ PETROLEUM COMPANY (IPC), WHICH GAVE IRAQ 50% OF THE PROFITS.[70] BUT THE IPC MAINTAINED A MONOPOLY ON EXPLORATION UNTIL 1961, WHEN QASIM PROCLAIMED LAW 80, TAKING BACK 99% OF THE IPC CONCESSION WITHOUT COMPENSATION.[71]

AND, IN 1960, QASIM ACTIVELY ENCOURAGED THE FOUNDATION OF THE ORGANIZATION OF PETROLEUM EXPORTING COUNTRIES — OPEC.[72]

 BY THE WAY, OPEC USHERED IN A NEW "GENRE" OF ANTI-ARAB CARTOONS, COMPLETE WITH HOOKED NOSES AND SINISTER BEARDS. ALMOST ALL ILLUSTRATE THE WEST'S DEPENDENCE ON THE GREEDY ARAB OIL SHEIKS. THEY REGULARLY APPEAR IN NEWSPAPERS—HERE ARE SOME OF MY FAVORITES.

FINALLY, QASIM CROSSED THE LINE WHEN HE REASSERTED IRAQ'S CLAIM OVER KUWAIT, AND THE BRITISH RESPONDED BY SENDING TROOPS TO PROTECT THEIR CLIENT STATE — A ROLE THE U.S. WOULD PLAY YEARS LATER.

MEANWHILE, KURDISH SEPARATISTS, UNDER THEIR LEADER MUSTAFA BARZANI, REVOLTED IN 1961 IN NORTHERN IRAQ. QASIM RESPONDED BY DEPLOYING THE IRAQI MILITARY TO THE AREA IN SEPTEMBER.

THIS WOULD NOT BE THE END OF BARZANI OR THE USE OF THE DESPERATE KURDS BY FOREIGN POWERS — IT IS A RUNNING THEME OF IRAQ'S HISTORY WHICH WE WILL RETURN TO LATER.

U.S. INVOLVEMENT IN IRAQ GOES BACK MANY YEARS. WAY BEFORE SADDAM WAS DECLARED THE NEW HITLER!

IN OCTOBER 1959, A GROUP OF BAATHISTS ATTEMPTED TO ASSASSINATE QASIM WITH THE HELP OF THE CIA. ONE OF THE ATTACKERS WAS A 25 YEAR OLD SADDAM HUSSEIN.[73,74,75]

ON FEB 8, 1963 THE CIA HELPED WITH THE BAATHIST COUP IN IRAQ. USING LISTS OF SUSPECTED COMMUNISTS PROVIDED BY THE CIA, PERHAPS THOUSANDS WERE KILLED.[76]

ROBERT KROMER, A NATIONAL SECURITY COUNCIL AIDE, WROTE TO KENNEDY THAT THE COUP WAS:

ALMOST CERTAINLY A GAIN FOR OUR SIDE.

JAMES H. CRITCHFIELD, CIA CHIEF OF ITS NEAR EAST AND SOUTH ASIA DIVISION, SAID:

WE REALLY HAD THE Ts CROSSED ON WHAT WAS HAPPENING, AND WE REGARDED IT AS A GREAT VICTORY.[77]

CRITCHFIELD STARTED HIS CAREER IN THE CIA IN 1948.

IT REPLACED THE OFFICE OF STRATEGIC SERVICES (OSS) WHEN HE WAS CHARGED WITH GATHERING INTELLIGENCE ABOUT THE SOVIET UNION.

HE USED THE INFAMOUS NAZI REINHARD GEHLEN, AND HIS "GEHLEN ORGANIZATION," WHICH WAS MADE UP OF MANY EX-NAZI WAR CRIMINALS.[78]

ALI SALEH SAADI, THE BAATH PARTY SECRETARY GENERAL, SAID OF THE COUP:

WE CAME TO POWER ON A CIA TRAIN.[79]

AFTER THE COUP, QASIM HAD A SWIFT TRIAL, AND WAS SHOT. HIS BODY WAS LATER SHOWN ON BAGHDAD TELEVISION.

AFTER MORE COUPS, AND POLITICAL MANEUVERING, 1968 BROUGT BAATHIST AHMED HASSAN AL BAKR TO POWER.

WHICH, IN TURN, BROUGHT HIS KINSMAN, SADDAM HUSSEIN, TO THE THRESHOLD OF POWER.

THE U.S. ABANDONED THE KURDISH INSURGENTS THEY PREVIOUSLY SUPPORTED AND SENT ARMS TO THE NEW REGIME.

WESTERN CORPORATIONS LIKE MOBILE, BECHTEL, AND BRITISH PETROLEUM, NOW BEGAN OPERATIONS IN IRAQ. THIS WAS THE FIRST MAJOR BUSINESS FOR AN AMERICAN FIRM IN IRAQ.[80]

ALSO, IN 1967, ANOTHER ARAB-ISRAELI WAR BROKE OUT.

WHICH WAS A DISASTER FOR THE ARAB COUNTRIES. ISRAEL ROUTED THE ARMIES OF EGYPT, JORDAN, & SYRIA, IN SIX DAYS.

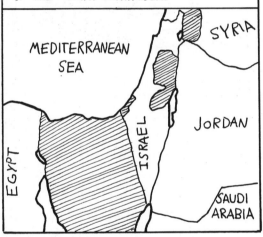

AND TOOK CONTROL OF THE WEST BANK, GAZA STRIP, THE GOLAN HEIGHTS, & THE SINAI PENINSULA.

MEDITERRANEAN SEA

SYRIA

EGYPT

ISRAEL

JORDAN

SAUDI ARABIA

THIS WAS A STUNNING BLOW TO THE SECULAR ARAB REGIMES.

IT OPENED THE DOOR MORE FULLY FOR THE RISE OF ISLAMIC FUNDAMENTALISM.

THE CONSERVATIVE ENEMIES OF THESE REGIMES BLAMED THE DEFEAT ON THEIR LACK OF PIETY. AYMAN AL ZAWAHIRI WAS A YOUNG MEMBER OF THE MUSLIM BROTHERHOOD IN EGYPT AT THE TIME. HE WOULD GO ON TO BE A MENTOR TO OSAMA BIN LADEN & HELP FOUND AL QAEDA.

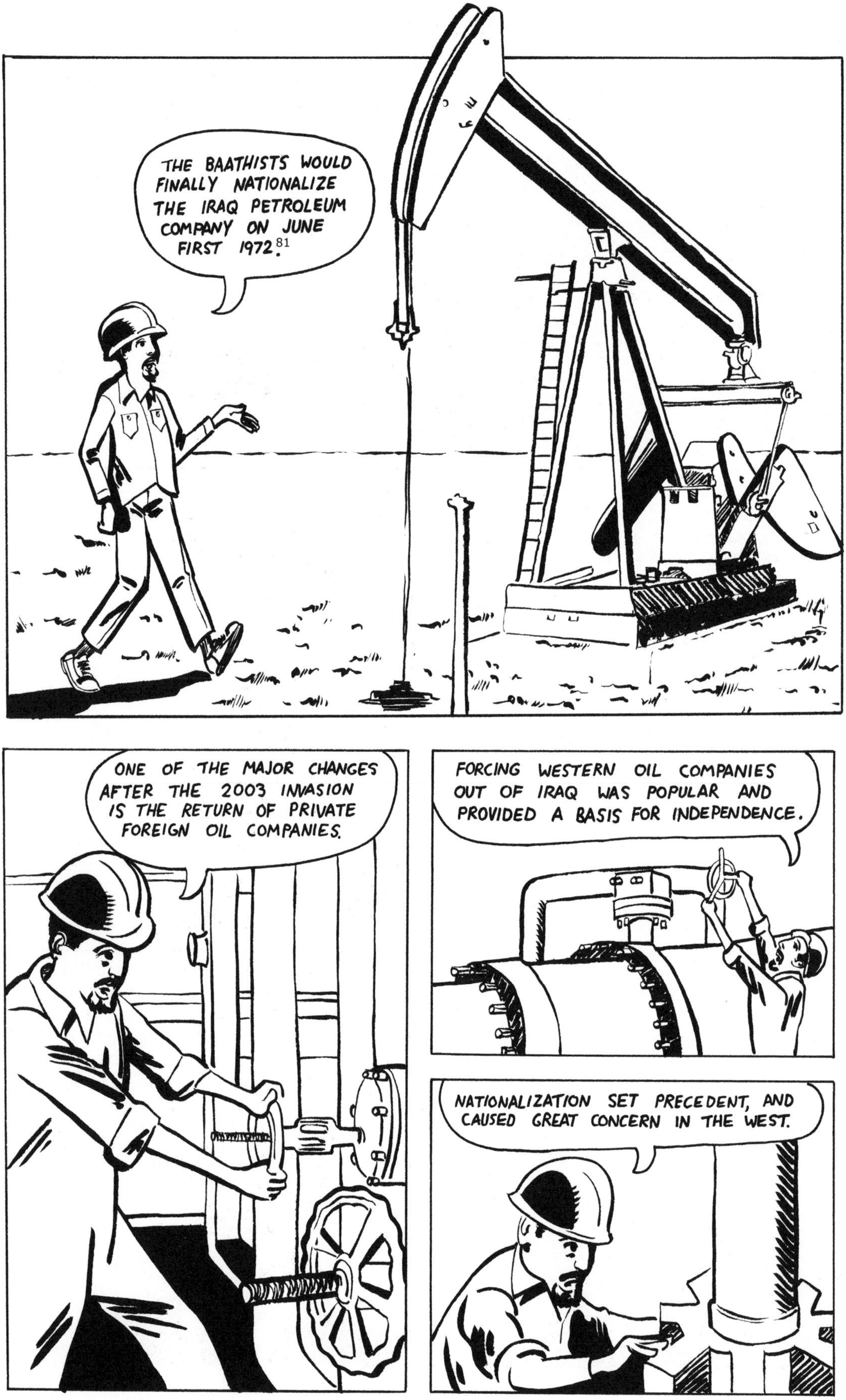
THE BAATHISTS WOULD FINALLY NATIONALIZE THE IRAQ PETROLEUM COMPANY ON JUNE FIRST 1972.[81]
ONE OF THE MAJOR CHANGES AFTER THE 2003 INVASION IS THE RETURN OF PRIVATE FOREIGN OIL COMPANIES.
FORCING WESTERN OIL COMPANIES OUT OF IRAQ WAS POPULAR AND PROVIDED A BASIS FOR INDEPENDENCE.
NATIONALIZATION SET PRECEDENT, AND CAUSED GREAT CONCERN IN THE WEST.

AROUND THIS TIME, IRAN (REMEMBER, A MAJOR U.S. ALLY AT THE TIME), AND SADDAM'S IRAQ WERE HAVING A BORDER DISPUTE OVER THE SHATT AL ARAB WATERWAY.

RECALL WHEN THE BRITISH CREATED IRAQ & CARVED OUT KUWAIT, DENYING IRAQ (AN OIL EXPORTER) IMPORTANT DEEP SEA PORTS.

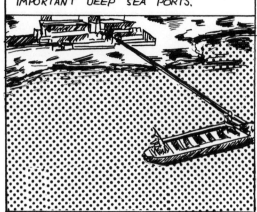

TO PUT PRESSURE ON SADDAM TO COME TO TERMS, THE U.S. AGAIN BEGAN TO ARM THE KURDS IN THE NORTH.[82]

THEN, IN 1975, IRAN AND IRAQ SETTLED THE DISPUTE WITH THE ALGIERS AGREEMENT.

THE U.S. PROMPLY (AGAIN) ABANDONED THE KURDISH REBELS.

COVERT ACTION SHOULD NOT BE CONFUSED WITH MISSIONARY WORK.[83]

THE U.S. WOULD CONTINUE THIS CYNICAL "NO WIN" STRATEGY THROUGHOUT ITS INVOLVEMENT IN THE MIDDLE EAST.

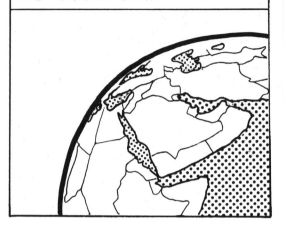

TO THE UNITED STATES, THIS WAS A POLITICAL CHESSBOARD.

REALPOLITIK[84] WAS EMPLOYED AND THE ECONOMIC & STRATEGIC INTRESTS OF THE U.S. WERE THE ONLY CONCERN.

THE IDEA OF INDEPENDENT REGIMES THAT HAD ANY MILITARY, OR STRATEGIC POWER, WAS TO BE PREVENTED AT ALL COSTS.

THAT'S ONE OF THE REASONS THE U.S. MADE SUCH A BIG DEAL OVER IRAN'S NUCLEAR PROGRAM.

NUCLEAR-ARMED IRAN WOULD PREVENT THE U.S. FROM ACTING FREELY IN THE MIDDLE EAST[85]

THE BAATHIST IDEOLOGY WAS POTENTIAL TROUBLE FOR THE ECONOMIC INTERESTS OF THE UNITED STATES.

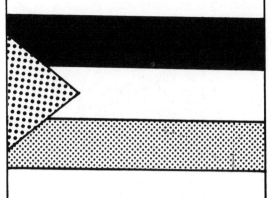

LIKE NASSERISM,[86] ANY MOVEMENT THAT NATIONALIZED RESOURCES AND UNIFIED NATIONS WOULD THREATEN CAPITALIST HEGEMONY.

BAATHISM CAME FROM MICHEL AFLAQ, A CHRISTIAN ARAB...

AND FROM SALAH AL BITAR, THEY FORMED THE ARAB SOCIALISM PARTY IN 1947.[87]

FOR A LITTLE WHILE, SYRIA & EGYPT FORMED A UNION CALLED THE UNITED ARAB REPUBLIC, BUT IT FAILED.

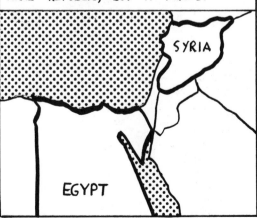

SYRIA

EGYPT

ANY POWERFUL GOVERNMENT THAT WOULD HAVE ALL THE RESOURCES OF THE REGION AT ITS DISPOSAL WOULD THREATEN THE STATUS QUO.

SO, ISLAMIC FUNDAMENTALISM WASN'T ALWAYS A BIG FORCE IN THE MIDDLE EAST.

THE SECULAR REGIMES WERE VERY SUCCESSFUL AT BRUTALLY SILENCING THEIR SECULAR OPPONENTS — THEIR RELIGIOUS OPPONENTS WERE MORE FORMIDABLE HOWEVER.

SAYYID QUTB, THE INTELLECTUAL OF THE MUSLIM BROTHERHOOD OF EGYPT, BECAME AN INSPIRATION OF ISLAMIC FUNDAMENTALISM.[88]

HE VISITED THE U.S. IN THE 1950s AND WAS SHOCKED TO SEE MEN AND WOMEN DANCING TOGETHER AT A CHURCH SPONSORED DANCE. HE THOUGHT THAT WESTERN STYLE FREEDOMS (OR THE ILLUSION OF FREEDOM) LEAD TO MORAL DECAY.

HE WENT BACK TO EGYPT CONVINCED THE WEST WAS EVIL.

IN EGYPT HE WAS ARRESTED WITH OTHER MEMBERS OF THE BROTHERHOOD.

QUTB WAS TORTURED BY CIA TRAINED SECURITY FORCES. THESE EXPERIENCES CONVINCED HIM OF THE CORRUPTION OF THE SECULAR REGIMES.[89,90]

QUTB WROTE AN INFLUENTIAL BOOK IN JAIL IN 1964. HIS IDEAS HELPED TO SHAPE THE RADICAL ISLAMIC MOVEMENT.

ONE TECHNIQUE THEY USED WAS TO RUB ANIMAL FAT ON PRISONERS' BODIES AND LET LOOSE VICIOUS DOGS ON THEM IN THE CELL.[91]

QUTB HAD A HEART ATTACK DURING ONE OF HIS TORTURE SESSIONS. HE SURVIVED ONLY TO BE EXECUTED LATER IN 1966.

IT'S IRONIC THAT TORTURE WAS A WEAPON IN THE "WAR ON TERROR" USED BY BOTH THE U.S...

AND ITS ALLIES IN THE MIDDLE EAST AGAINST POLITICAL OPPONENTS AND INNOCENT PEOPLE.

DETAINEES WERE SOMETIMES SENT TO PLACES LIKE EGYPT & JORDAN TO BE TORTURED. THEY CALLED THIS "EXTRAORDINARY RENDITION."[92]

AN EXAMPLE: THE CIA KIDNAPPED HASSAN MUSTAFA OSAMA NASR FROM THE STREET IN MILAN, THEN HE WAS FLOWN TO EGYPT WHERE HE WAS TORTURED. HE WAS SOON RELEASED BECAUSE HE WAS INNOCENT.[93]

ROBERT SELDON LADY,[94] FORMER CIA CHIEF IN MILAN, SAID OF NASR'S ABDUCTION:

OF COURSE IT WAS AN ILLEGAL OPERATION. BUT THAT'S OUR JOB. WE'RE AT WAR AGAINST TERRORISM.[95]

ALVIN BERNARD "BUZZY" KRONGARD, FORMER CIA DIRECTOR SAID:

THAT'S TORTURE. I'M COMFORTABLE WITH SAVING THAT.[96]

THE MEDIA WAS COMPLICIT WITH THE TORTURE PROGRAM. MANY OUTLETS REFERRED TO THE PROGRAM AS "ENHANCED INTERROGATIONS."

IT WASN'T UNTIL AUGUST OF 2014 THAT THE NEW YORK TIMES EVEN STARTED USING THE WORD TORTURE.[97]

PRESIDENT OBAMA EVEN SAID THAT AFTER 9/11 THE U.S.

TORTURED SOME FOLKS.[98]

ACCORING TO A SENATE REPORT, CIA'S METHODS LIKE WATERBOARDING, & OTHER TECHNIQUES ON CAPTURED MILITANTS, DIDN'T PRODUCE ANY COUNTER-TERRORISM BREAKTHROUGHS.[99]

COLIN POWELL, SECRETARY OF STATE AT THE TIME, DIDN'T EVEN KNOW ABOUT THE PROGRAM AT FIRST.[100]

DICK CHENEY WAS ASKED ABOUT HOW HE FELT ABOUT INNOCENT PEOPLE BEING TORTURED, HE SAID IN 2014:

I HAVE NO PROBLEM AS LONG AS WE ACHIEVE OUR OBJECTIVE.[101]

THE "WAR ON TERRORISM" HAS ITS IDEOLOGICAL ROOTS IN THE WESTERN COUNTERPART OF THE MUSLIM BROTHERHOOD: THE NEO CONSERVATIVES. BOTH GROUPS BELIEVED IN THE FIGHT BETWEEN GOOD AND EVIL.

UNLIKE SOMEONE LIKE HENRY KISSINGER, WHO BELIEVED IN REALPOLITIK...

THE NEOCONS WERE IDEOLOGUES.

THE TEACHINGS OF LEO STRAUSS, A UNIVERSITY OF CHICAGO PROFESSOR, BECAME THE INTELLECTUAL FOUNDATION OF WHAT BECAME THE NEOCONSERVATIVE MOVEMENT.[102]

AMONG HIS DISCIPLES WERE PAUL WOLFOWITZ, WHO BECAME A DEPUTY SECRETARY OF DEFENSE, WILLIAM KRISTOL, EDITOR OF THE WEEKLY STANDARD, AND FRANCIS FUKUYAMA, AUTHOR.

THE SMALL CLUSTER OF ADVISERS IN GEORGE W. BUSH'S ADMINISTRATION JOKINGLY THEMSELVES CALLED "THE CABAL."[103]

MANY OF THE NEOCONS WERE FORMER LIBERALS. IRVING KRISTOL SAID, AFTER PROGRESSIVE LAWS WERE PASSED IN THE 1960s & 1970s :

WOULD YOU SAY CRIME WOULD GO UP? DRUG ADDICTION WOULD GO UP? ILLEGITIMACY WOULD GO UP? OR WILL THEY GO DOWN? EVERYONE WOULD HAVE SAID THEY WOULD GO DOWN, & EVERYONE WOULD HAVE BEEN WRONG.[104]

BOTH THE ISLAMIC FUNDAMENTALISTS & THE NEOCONS SAW THE INDIVIDUAL FREEDOMS OF THE 1960s LEADING TO MORAL RELATIVISM & NIHILISM IN THE WEST AS A MAIN PROBLEM.

FOR STRAUS, THE ANSWER WAS TO CREATE MYTHS TO GALVINIZE AND MOTIVATE PEOPLE.

FOR QUTB, THE ANSWER WAS TO TURN TOWARDS PURITANICAL ISLAM.

NECESSARY ILLUSIONS, LIKE MAJOR THREATS TO AMERICA, OR MYTHS LIKE THE USA HAD A UNIQUE DESTINY TO BATTLE EVIL LIKE COMMUNISM (THEN LATER, ISLAM) WERE PROMOTED.

NOW BOTH SIDES USE FEAR TO RALLY PEOPLE AROUND THEM.[105]

NOT JUST FEAR BUT THE ILLUSION OF FEAR. FOR THE ISLAMISTS, IT IS THE WESTERNERS CORRUPT INFIDEL AGENDA TO PERVERT ISLAM.

FOR THE WEST IT IS A RUTHLESS ORGANIZED WORLDWIDE PLOT TO DESTROY AMERICA.

JUST AS MANY OF STRAUSS'S FOLLOWERS WOULD REAPPEAR IN PROMINENT POSITIONS IN WASHINGTON YEARS LATER...

MANY OF QUTB'S FOLLOWERS WOULD REAPPEAR IN THE MIDDLE EAST AS ENEMIES OF AMERICA.

FROM THE 1950s THROUGH THE 1970s, THE UNITED STATES WAS MOSTLY FOCUSED ON THE COLD WAR BUT THAT WOULD CHANGE AS THE MIDDLE EAST BECAME INCREASINGLY VITAL TO THE WORLD ECONOMY.

AND IN THE 1970s, THE MIDDLE EAST BECAME MORE IMPORTANT THAN EVER FOR THE AMERICANS.

THE 1973 OIL EMBARGO DURING THE YOM KIPPUR WAR BETWEEN ISRAEL & SYRIA / EGYPT TAUGHT THE UNITED STATES A LESSON.

ARAB STATES REFUSED TO SELL OIL TO AMERICA WHO STEPPED IN ON THE SIDE OF ISRAEL WITH CRUCIAL ARMS SHIPMENTS.[106]

THE WORLD ECONOMY WAS SHAKEN BY THE EMBARGO, AND THERE WAS FEAR OF AN ECONOMIC DISRUPTION.[107] THE WORLD MARKET DEPENDED ON THE FLOW OF OIL. ANY INTERRUPTION COULD DAMAGE ECONOMIES.

BY THE 1980s, THE ARAB REGIMES HAD BECOME MUCH WEALTHIER. IRAQ'S 1968 OIL REVENUES WERE 476 MILLION. IN 1980, THEY WERE 26 BILLION. "PETRO-DOLLARS" FLOODED THE GULF.[108]

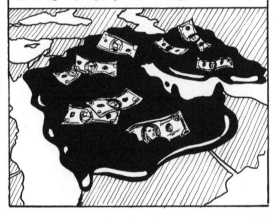

THE U.S. WAS ONLY SURPASSED IN OIL PRODUCTION BY THE MIDDLE EAST IN 1968.[109]

NEVER AGAIN WOULD THE U.S. ALLOW ACCESS TO OIL FROM THE GULF TO STOP. THIS BECAME PART OF THE NATIONAL SECURITY PRIORITY OF AMERICA.[110]

THIS MIGHT HELP EXPLAIN WHY THE MIDDLE EAST IS SUCH A MESS. OFTEN, WE HEAR TALK OF ANCIENT, CULTURAL, AGE-OLD, RELIGIOUS RIVALRIES AS THE SOURCE OF CONFLICT AND INSTABILITY.

ISRAELIS & PALESTINIANS HAVE LEGITIMATE CONCERNS & GRIEVANCES. ONE SIDE IS JEWISH & THE OTHER IS LARGELY MUSLIM. RELIGION MAY PLAY A ROLE, BUT RESOURCES AND LAND ARE THE REASONS FOR THE CONFLICT.

AND AMERICA IS ALSO INTERESTED IN SECURING OIL & NATURAL GAS. IT IS NOT A WAR AGAINST "RADICAL ISLAM," BUT A WAR FOR RESOURCES. THE INDIGENOUS PEOPLES' FAITH IS IRRELEVANT.

AND SOON, THE FIGHT IN THE MIDDLE EAST WILL BE OVER THE MOST ELEMENTAL OF ALL RESOURCES: WATER.

TODAY, A GALLON OF CLEAN WATER COSTS MORE THAN A GALLON OF GAS.[111]

CONSIDERING THE POLITICAL INSTABILITY & CLIMATE CHANGE, THIS ALREADY ARID PART OF THE WORLD WILL SEE MORE CONFLICT OVER WATER.

POW
POW

BY THE WAY, IT'S NOT JUST THE MIDDLE EAST WHERE WATER IS AN ISSUE. THERE WAS A RECENT FIVE-YEAR DROUGHT IN CALIFORNIA.

ALTHOUGH THE DROUGHT WAS OVER IN 2017, WATER AVAILABILITY IS NOW A MAJOR ISSUE IN CALIFORNIA.

AND IT DID NOT EXACTLY BRING OUT THE BEST IN PEOPLE. A WEALTHY RESIDENT OF RANCHO SANTA FE, CALIFORNIA SAID:

PEOPLE "SHOULD NOT BE FORCED TO LIVE ON PROPERTY WITH BROWN LAWNS, GOLF ON BROWN COURSES." & "WE PAY SIGNIFICANT PROPERTY TAXES BASED ON WHERE WE LIVE" ADDING: "AND, NO, WE'RE NOT EQUAL WHEN IT COMES TO WATER."

THIS IS SIMILAR TO THE SITUATION IN THE WEST BANK. WATER IS DIVERTED TO THE ISRAELI SETTLERS' GREEN LAWNS & BACK YARD POOLS, WHILE PALESTINIAN NEIGHBORS STRUGGLE DAILY WITH WATER SHORTAGES.[112]

THE POLICY OF THE U.S. GOVERNMENT DURING THE COLD WAR BECAME FAMILIAR. FIRST, SUPPORT ANY REGIMES THAT WERE NOT NATIONALIST OR REMOTELY LEFTIST.

THEN, RUTHLESSLY PURSUE ITS ECONOMIC INTERESTS ANYWHERE AND EVERYWHERE.

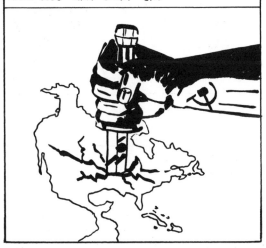

IT WASN'T CLEAR THAT THE USA WOULD WIN THE COLD WAR EARLY ON.

BUT THESE POLICIES WOULD EVENTUALLY BEAR FRUIT FOR THE AMERICANS.

AND, THERE ARE MANY FACTIONS IN WASHINGTON THAT COMPETE FOR INFLUENCE, SO NOT EVERYONE AGREES ON WHAT CONSTITUTES AMERICA'S "INTERESTS."

THE RIVALRY WITH THE SOVIETS RESTRICTED AMERICA'S ACTIONS IN THE 20TH CENTURY, BUT IT WOULD END IN VICTORY FOR THE USA. THE BENEFITS OF VICTORY WERE SECURED BY THE GROUNDWORK LAID BY MILITARY & CIA ACTIONS BEFORE-HAND.

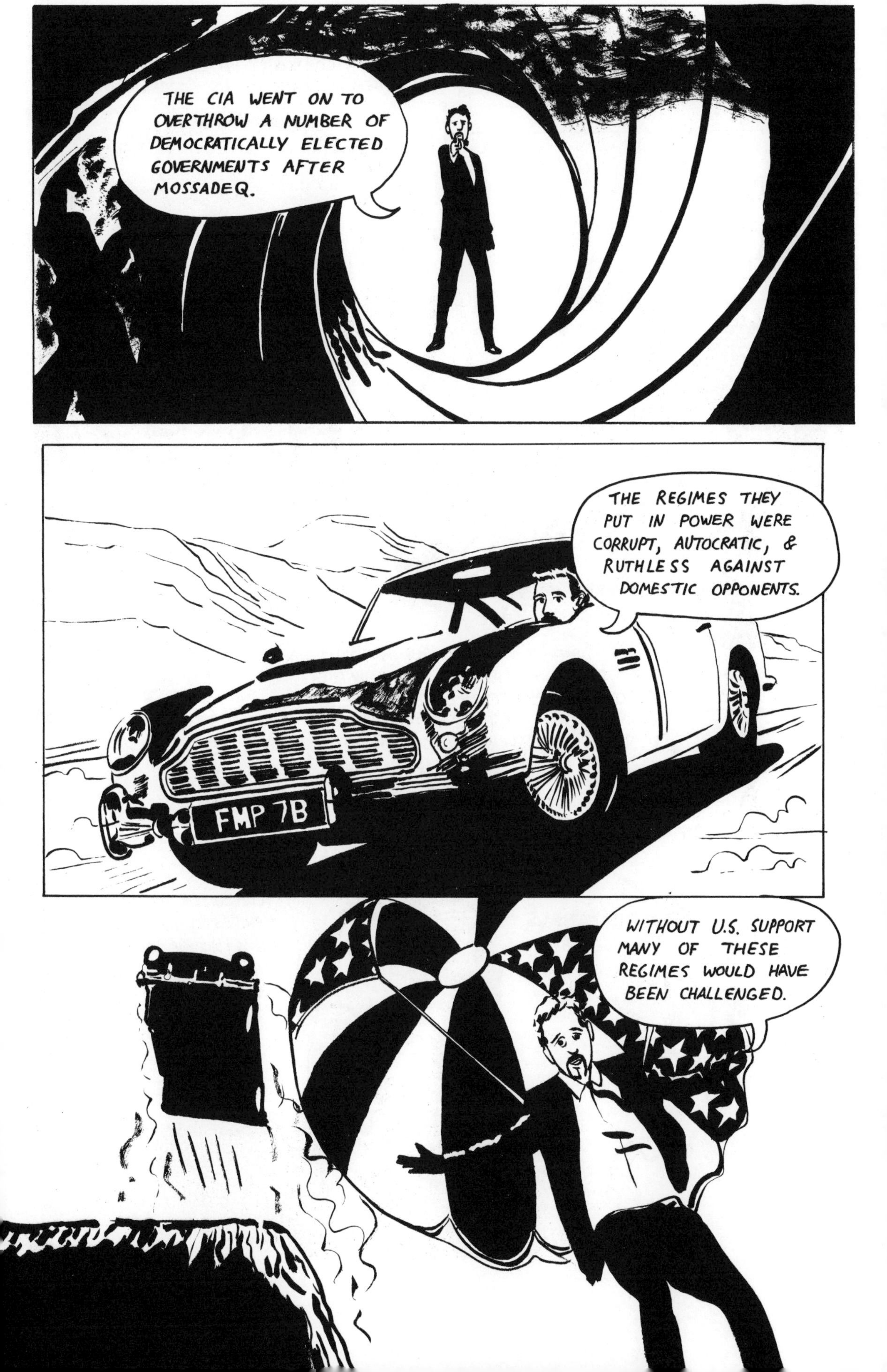
THE CIA WENT ON TO OVERTHROW A NUMBER OF DEMOCRATICALLY ELECTED GOVERNMENTS AFTER MOSSADEQ.
THE REGIMES THEY PUT IN POWER WERE CORRUPT, AUTOCRATIC, & RUTHLESS AGAINST DOMESTIC OPPONENTS.
FMP 7B
WITHOUT U.S. SUPPORT MANY OF THESE REGIMES WOULD HAVE BEEN CHALLENGED.

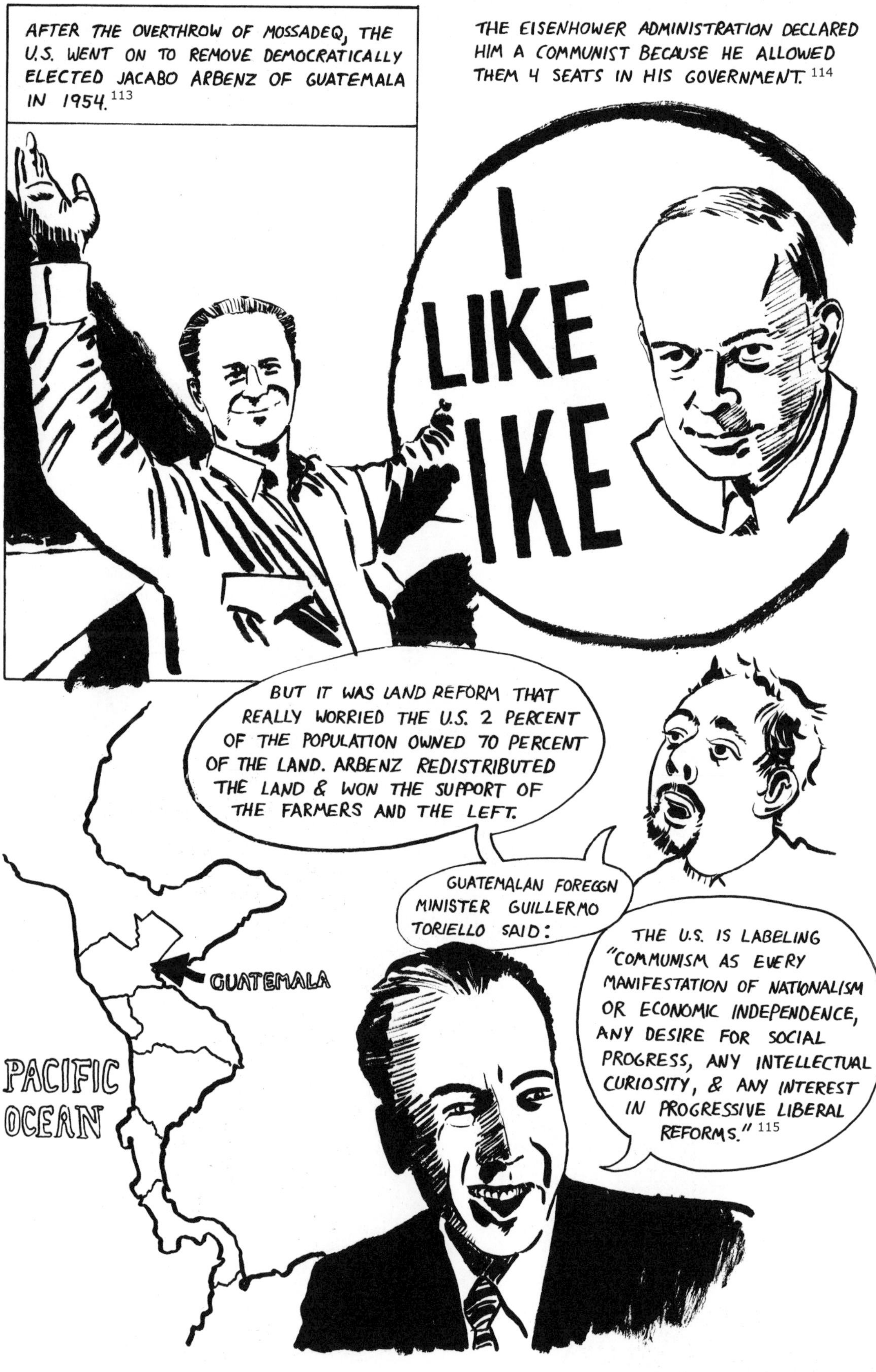
AFTER THE OVERTHROW OF MOSSADEQ, THE U.S. WENT ON TO REMOVE DEMOCRATICALLY ELECTED JACABO ARBENZ OF GUATEMALA IN 1954.[113]
THE EISENHOWER ADMINISTRATION DECLARED HIM A COMMUNIST BECAUSE HE ALLOWED THEM 4 SEATS IN HIS GOVERNMENT.[114]
I LIKE IKE
BUT IT WAS LAND REFORM THAT REALLY WORRIED THE U.S. 2 PERCENT OF THE POPULATION OWNED 70 PERCENT OF THE LAND. ARBENZ REDISTRIBUTED THE LAND & WON THE SUPPORT OF THE FARMERS AND THE LEFT.
GUATEMALAN FOREGGN MINISTER GUILLERMO TORIELLO SAID:
THE U.S. IS LABELING "COMMUNISM AS EVERY MANIFESTATION OF NATIONALISM OR ECONOMIC INDEPENDENCE, ANY DESIRE FOR SOCIAL PROGRESS, ANY INTELLECTUAL CURIOSITY, & ANY INTEREST IN PROGRESSIVE LIBERAL REFORMS."[115]
GUATEMALA
PACIFIC OCEAN

IN THE FOLLOWING DECADES, UNDER THE GUISE OF COUNTER-INSURGENCY, THE U.S. & ISRAEL SUPPORTED THE RIGHT-WING GOVERNMENT'S CAMPAIGN OF TERROR.[116]

IN ONE OF THE WORST GENOCIDAL CAMPAIGNS EVER, MORE THAN 600 MAYAN VILLAGES IN THE COUNTRYSIDE WERE DESTROYED BY THE ARMY. ABOUT 200,000 PEOPLE WERE KILLED, THE MAJORITY WERE CIVILIANS.[117]

UNDER JIMMY CARTER, THE SUPPORT & TRAINING FOR GUATEMALA'S MILITARY WAS CHANNELED THROUGH ISRAEL.

IN THE 70s & 80s "ISRAEL HAD BECOME [GUATEMALA'S] MAIN PROVIDER OF TRAINING, LIGHT & HEAVY ARSENALS OF WEAPONRY, AIRCRAFT, [....] & OTHER VITAL ASSISTANCE."[118]

EFRAIN RIOS MONTT WAS "OUR GUY" AS PRESIDENT OF GUATEMALA DURING THE CRESCENDO OF VIOLENCE IN 1982-83.

A LAWYER FROM A TEAM INVESTIGATING ATROCITIES IN GUATEMALA WROTE, "THE GOVERNMENT CARRIED OUT VIRTUALLY INDISCRIMINATE MURDER OF MEN, WOMEN, AND CHILDREN." AND THAT CHILDREN WERE, "THROWN INTO BURNING HOMES. THEY ARE THROWN IN THE AIR AND SPEARED WITH BAYONETS. WE HEARD MANY, MANY STORIES OF CHILDREN BEING PICKED UP BY THE ANKLES AND SWUNG AGAINST POLES SO THEIR HEADS ARE DESTROYED." [119]

RONALD REAGAN SAID RIOS MONTT WAS:

A MAN OF "GREAT PERSONAL INTEGRITY" [AND WAS] "GETTING A BUM RAP" FROM HUMAN RIGHTS ACTIVISTS. [120]

WHEN THE COUP HAPPENED IN 1954, A YOUNG ARGENTINEAN DOCTOR WAS AMONG MANY OF THE PEOPLE SWEPT UP IN THE REPRESSION AFTERWARDS.

ERNESTO GUEVARA BECAME CONVINCED THAT "YANKEE IMPERIALISM" WAS RESPONSIBILE, & THAT ARMED REVOLUTION WAS THE ONLY WAY TOWARDS FREEDOM.

HE WOULD GO ON TO BECOME PART OF FIDEL CASTRO'S BAND OF GUERRILLA FIGHTERS, & PLAY A BIG PART IN THE CUBAN REVOLUTION.

HE WAS KILLED IN 1964 IN BOLIVIA WHILE TRYING TO LEAD A REVOLT. THE CIA PLAYED A ROLE IN HIS CAPTURE & SUBSEQUENT ASSASSINATION.[121]

INDONESIA IS THE MOST POPULOUS MUSLIM STATE IN THE WORLD.

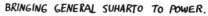
Pacific Ocean

AND, IN 1965 THE INDONESIAN MILITARY, WITH THE SUPPORT OF THE U.S./CIA, OVERTHREW THE DEMOCRATICALLY ELECTED PRESIDENT SUKARNO.

BRINGING GENERAL SUHARTO TO POWER.

SUHARTO'S "ARMY LATER ENCOURAGED & JOINED IN A NATIONWIDE MASSACRE OF KNOWN & SUSPECTED COMMUNISTS, WHICH THE CIA HAS SAID CLAIMED 250,000 LIVES." ONE OF THE WORST MASS KILLINGS OF THE 20TH CENTURY.[122]

SUKARNO ALLOWED THE COMMUNIST PARTY (PKI) TO PARTICIPATE IN THE GOVERNMENT, & THAT IRRITATED THE U.S. THE CIA PROVIDED LISTS OF COMMUNISTS TO THE ARMY DURING THE KILLING.

PARTY KOMMUNIST INDONESIA (P.K.I.)

SALVADOR ALLENDE WAS DEMOCRATICALLY ELECTED PRESIDENT OF CHILE, & ON SEPTEMBER 11, 1973, HE WAS OVERTHROWN, AGAIN, WITH THE AID OF THE CIA.[123]

2% OF THE POPULATION HAD 46% OF THE INCOME. ALLENDE'S REFORMS: NATIONALIZATION OF INDUSTRIES & AGRARIAN REFORM.

I DON'T SEE WHY WE NEED TO STAND BY & WATCH A COUNTRY GO COMMUNIST BECAUSE OF THE IRRESPONSIBILITY OF ITS OWN PEOPLE.*

GEN. PINOCHET CAME TO POWER, AND IN "TWO YEARS WIPED OUT 30,000 OF THE POPULATION & IMPRISONED 200,000."[124]

*ACTUAL QUOTE FROM NOBEL PRIZE WINNER HENRY KISSINGER.

"IN THE UNITED STATES, AS YOU KNOW, WE ARE SYMPATHETIC WITH WHAT YOU ARE TRYING TO DO HERE."[125]

ONE WITNESS SAID: "THEY TOOK VICTOR TO THE TABLE & ORDERED HIM TO PUT HIS HANDS ON IT. IN THE HANDS OF THE OFFICER ROSE, SWIFTLY, AN AXE. WITH A SINGLE STROKE HE SEVERED THE FINGERS ON VICTOR'S LEFT HAND, & WITH ANOTHER STROKE, THE FINGERS OF THE RIGHT. [HE THEN BEAT] HIM WHILE SHOUTING: 'NOW SING, YOU MOTHERFUCKER, NOW SING.'"[127]

VICTOR JARRA WAS A FOLK SINGER WHO SANG ABOUT SOCIAL JUSTICE. HE WAS ONE OF THE THOUSANDS SWEPT UP AFTER THE COUP.[126]

IN 1979 THE IRANIAN REVOLUTION BROKE OUT.

THEN THERE WAS THE SOVIET INVASION OF AFGHANISTAN.

AND THE SANDINISTA REVOLUTION IN NICARAGUA.

AFTER THE U.S. LOSS IN VIETNAM IN 1973...

AND AS A RESULT OF THE WATERGATE INVESTIGATION THE SAME YEAR...

THE CHURCH COMMITTEE WAS FORMED IN THE SENATE. IT WAS NAMED AFTER SENATOR CHURCH, & IT INVESTIGATED UNCONSTITUTIONAL ACTIONS CARRIED OUT BY U.S. INTELLIGENCE AGENCIES.

INVESTIGATORS REVEALED THE NSA'S PROJETS SHAMROCK & MINARET - PROGRAMS THAT MONITORED WIRE COMMUNICATIONS TO & FROM THE U.S.[130]

HELLO? WHO IS THIS?

THE FINAL REPORT SAID, SINCE THE 1940s, AND CONTINUING THROUGH THE EARLY 1970s, "INTELLIGENCE EXCESSES, AT HOME & ABROAD," WEREN'T THE "PRODUCT OF ANY SINGLE PARTY," BUT OCCURRED AS THE U.S. BECAME A WORLD POWER.[128, 129]

THEY ALSO DELVED INTO THE FBI'S DOMESTIC SPYING PROGRAM CALLED COINTELPRO, WHICH WAS A PROJECT OF "COVERT ACTIONS DESIGNED TO DISRUPT AND DISCREDIT" THE ACTIVITIES OF GROUPS AND INDIVIDUALS DEEMED A THREAT TO SOCIAL ORDER, E.G. ELECTED OFFICIALS, ANTI-WAR GROUPS, EVEN MARTIN LUTHER KING.[131]

LAWS WERE PASSED TO CHECK THE POWER OF INTELLIGENCE ORGANIZATIONS, AND A COMMITTEE ON INTELLIGENCE WAS ESTABLISHED. IN 1978, JIMMY CARTER SIGNED THE FOREIGN INTELLIGENCE SURVEILLANCE ACT (FISA).

THIS REQUIRED WARRANTS FOR WIRETAPS BUT, IN THE EARLY 2000s, GEORGE BUSH & THE NSA IGNORED THE LAW WITH A WARRANTLESS PROGRAM.[132]

I SAID WHO IS THIS?!

THEN IN 2013, FORMER NSA EMPLOYEE JOHN SNOWDEN, REVEALED A SECRET PROGRAM THAT COLLECTED PERSONAL COMPUTER DATA FROM PRACTICALLY EVERY AMERICAN CITIZEN.[133]
SNOWDEN RELEASED DOCUMENTS THAT SHOWED THE ILLEGAL PROGRAM SPIED, NOT ONLY ON CIVILIANS, BUT ALSO ON LEADERS OF OTHER NATIONS, LIKE GERMANY'S ANGELA MERKEL.

SPYING BETWEEN FRIENDS — THAT'S JUST NOT DONE.[134]

THE REAGAN ADMINISTRATION CONTINUED AMERICAN INVOLVEMENT IN OTHER COUNTRIES. THE U.S. ILLEGALLY SOLD WEAPONS TO IRAN VIA ISRAEL IN EXCHANGE FOR THE RELEASE OF HOSTAGES HELD IN LEBANON BY SHIA MILITIA.[135]

A FACTION IN THE AMERICAN GOVERNMENT, LED BY OLIVER NORTH AND THE CIA, TOOK PROFITS FROM THE ARMS SALES & USED THEM TO FUND THE COUNTER-REVOLUTIONARIES IN NICARAGUA.[136]

AGAINST DOMESTIC AND INTERNATIONAL LAW, THE U.S. SUPPORTED THESE CONTRAS, WHO COMMITTED MASSACRES, RAPE, AND OTHER CRIMES AGAINST THE CIVILIAN POPULATION.[137]

ONE ATROCITY WAS AGAINST RICARDO BUSTILLO, A CATHOLIC ACTIVIST, AND HIS 5 CHILDREN. HE & HIS KIDS WERE DRAGGED OUT OF THEIR HOUSE, & THE MUTILATED BODIES OF THE CHILDREN WERE FOUND THE NEXT MORNING BY THEIR MOM. BUSTILLO'S BODY WAS FOUND LATER.[138]

THE CONTRAS ARE THE MORAL EQUIVALENT OF OUR FOUNDING FATHERS.[139]

MONEY FROM ILLEGAL DRUG SHIPMENTS INTO THE U.S. WAS ANOTHER SOURCE OF FUNDING FOR THE CONTRAS.[140, 141]

ACCORDING TO A SERIES OF ARTICLES BY GARY WEBB IN 1996 IN THE SAN JOSE MERCURY NEWS, THE U.S. WAS AT LEAST COMPLICIT IN DRUG TRAFFICKING.[142]

ACCORDING TO WEBB, THE CIA HELPED SPARK THE CRACK EPIDEMIC IN THE LATE 1980s AND EARLY 1990s.[143]

COCAINE WAS SHIPPED INTO SAN FRANCISCO, AND DISTRIBUTED IN CALIFORNIA BY A NICARAGUAN NAMED DANILO BLANDON.[144]

HE SOLD DRUGS TO A STREET DEALER KNOWN AS "FREEWAY" RICK ROSS, WHO USED LA GANGS, THE CRIPS, & BLOODS, AS SELLERS. HE BECAME A CRACK KINGPIN.[145]

CONGRESSWOMAN MAXINE WATERS SAID THAT THE ALLIANCE BETWEEN THE CONTRAS, DRUG DEALERS, & INTELLIGENCE AGENCIES WAS:

ONE OF THE WORST OFFICIAL ABUSES IN OUR NATION'S HISTORY.[146]

AROUND THE SAME TIME, THE UNITED STATES BEGAN FUNDING THE ANTI-SOVIET MUJAHIDEEN IN AFGHANISTAN.

NOT SURPRISINGLY, THE CIA ALSO USED DRUGS (OPIUM), AS A WEAPON & SOURCE OF FINANCE FOR THEIR OPERATIONS THERE TOO.[147]

THE FRENCH HEAD OF FOREIGN INTELLIGENCE PROPOSED TO RONALD REAGAN THE IDEA OF MAKING DRUGS SEIZED BY THE DEA AVAILABLE TO RUSSIAN SOLDIERS DURING THE WAR IN ORDER TO WEAKEN THEM.[148]

REAGAN THOUGHT IT WAS A GREAT IDEA AND THE CIA CHIEF WILLIAM CASEY "LOVED IT... HE LEAPED FROM HIS CHAIR AND SLICED AT THE AIR WITH HIS FISTS."[149]

IT'S NOT CLEAR IF "OPERATION MOSQUITO" WAS CARRIED OUT BY THE CIA, BUT DRUG ADDICTION WAS A HUGE ISSUE THE RUSSIAN ARMY BROUGHT BACK TO RUSSIA WHERE IT WAS, AND IS, A BIG PROBLEM.[150]

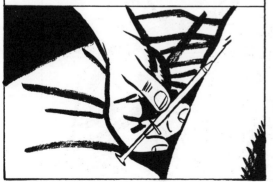

FROM 1979 TO THE 1990s, HEROIN ON THE WORLD MARKET ROSE TEN TIMES THE LEVEL IT WAS BEFORE THE WAR. IRONICALLY, IT WAS DURING THE REAGAN ADMINISTRATION THAT THE "WAR ON DRUGS" BEGAN, AND HIS WIFE FAMOUSLY TOLD KIDS TO:

JUST SAY NO.

SPEAKING OF DRUGS, HASSAN AL SABBAH COMMANDED AN ISLAMIC SECT IN PERSIA THAT FOUGHT THE CRUSADERS IN THE 11TH CENTURY. THEY ARE REMEMBERED TODAY AS "ASSASSINS."[151]

MEDIEVAL EUROPEANS MADE UP MANY LEGENDS ABOUT AL SABBAH AND HIS FOLLOWERS, LIKE ATTRIBUTING THEIR FIERCENESS IN BATTLE TO THE INFLUENCE OF DRUGS LIKE HASHISH. MARCO POLO POPULARIZED THE LEGEND.[152]

THESE "CRAZED WARRIORS" CAME TO BE CALLED HASHISHEEN, WHICH IS WHERE THE ENGLISH WORD ASSASSIN COMES FROM.

THE ASSASSINS! MAD SLAYERS OF THE EAST!

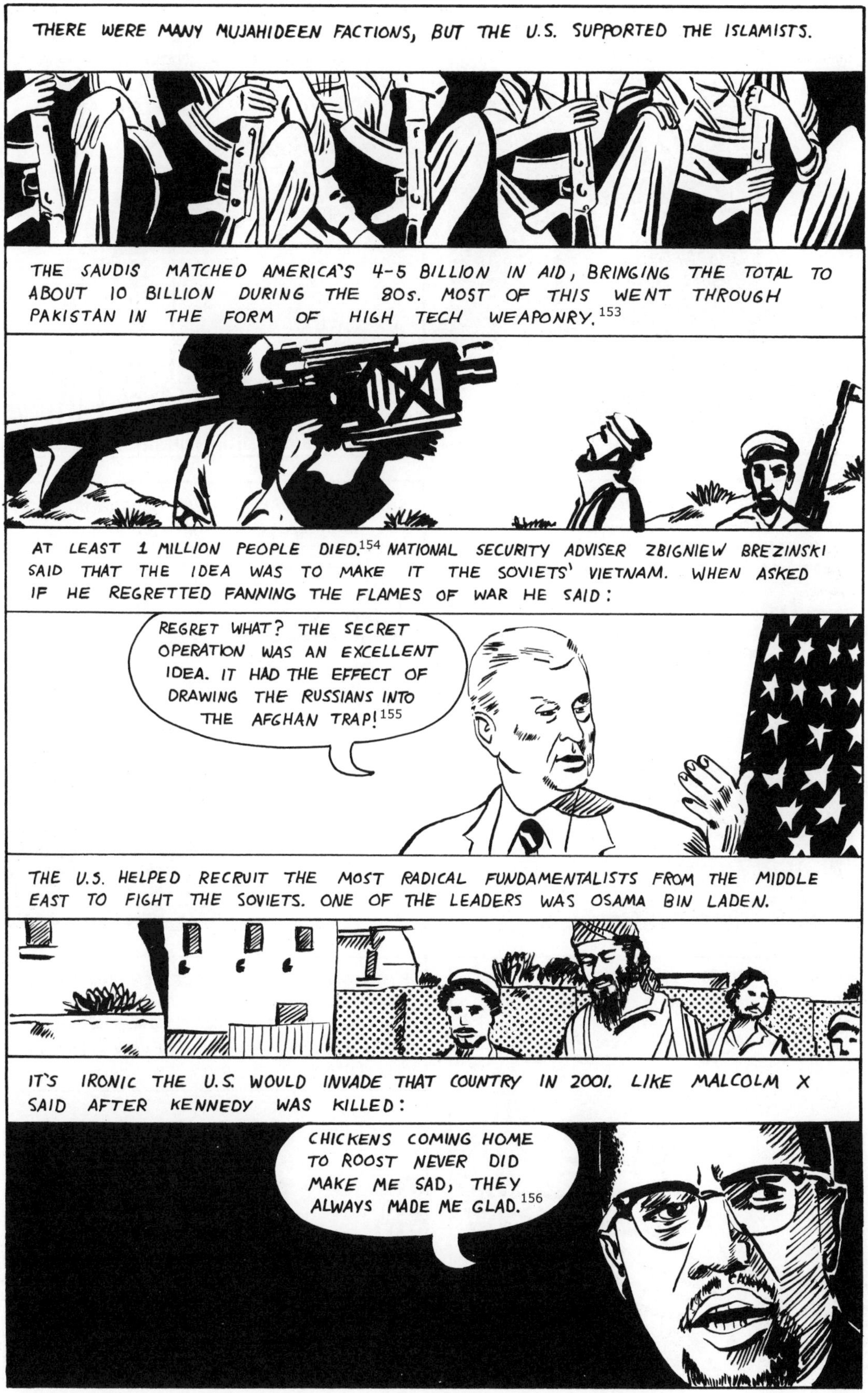
THERE WERE MANY MUJAHIDEEN FACTIONS, BUT THE U.S. SUPPORTED THE ISLAMISTS.
THE SAUDIS MATCHED AMERICA'S 4-5 BILLION IN AID, BRINGING THE TOTAL TO ABOUT 10 BILLION DURING THE 80s. MOST OF THIS WENT THROUGH PAKISTAN IN THE FORM OF HIGH TECH WEAPONRY.[153]
AT LEAST 1 MILLION PEOPLE DIED.[154] NATIONAL SECURITY ADVISER ZBIGNIEW BREZINSKI SAID THAT THE IDEA WAS TO MAKE IT THE SOVIETS' VIETNAM. WHEN ASKED IF HE REGRETTED FANNING THE FLAMES OF WAR HE SAID:
REGRET WHAT? THE SECRET OPERATION WAS AN EXCELLENT IDEA. IT HAD THE EFFECT OF DRAWING THE RUSSIANS INTO THE AFGHAN TRAP![155]
THE U.S. HELPED RECRUIT THE MOST RADICAL FUNDAMENTALISTS FROM THE MIDDLE EAST TO FIGHT THE SOVIETS. ONE OF THE LEADERS WAS OSAMA BIN LADEN.
IT'S IRONIC THE U.S. WOULD INVADE THAT COUNTRY IN 2001. LIKE MALCOLM X SAID AFTER KENNEDY WAS KILLED:
CHICKENS COMING HOME TO ROOST NEVER DID MAKE ME SAD, THEY ALWAYS MADE ME GLAD.[156]

PROFESSOR WARD CHURCHILL MADE SIMILAR COMMENTS AFTER 9/11.

HE WROTE "SOME PEOPLE PUSH BACK: ON THE JUSTICE OF ROOSTING CHICKENS." CHURCHILL SAID THE ATTACKS WERE A RESPONSE TO THE HISTORY OF ABUSES.

CHURCHILL SAID THOSE KILLED IN THE WORLD TRADE CENTER WERE "A TECHNOCRATIC CORPS AT THE VERY HEART OF AMERICA'S GLOBAL FINANCIAL EMPIRE," & HE CALLED THEM "LITTLE EICHMANNS".[157, 158]

GEORGE PATAKI, THEN GOVERNOR OF NEW YORK, CALLED CHURCHILL:

A BIGOTED TERRORIST SUPPORTER.

HE WAS FIRED BY UNIVERSITY OFFICIALS WHO ALLEGED "RESEARCH MISCONDUCT."[159]

PHILOSOPHER TED HONDERICH WROTE: "AMERICANS, BECAUSE OF THEIR UNIQUE RELATIONSHIP TO POWER, HAVE A MORAL OBJECTIVE TO THINK CAREFULLY" [ABOUT U.S. POLICY].[160]

94

THE "WAR ON TERROR" ALSO OPENED UP AN ORWELLIAN APPROACH TO PROTECTING THE INTERESTS OF THE UNITED STATES AND ITS ALLIES.

INCLUDING RACIAL PROFILING OF THE ARAB AND MUSLIM COMMUNITY, AND ...

ARRESTS OF MISGUIDED YOUTHS BY THE FBI, LIKE ADEL DAOUD, WHO WAS GIVEN A FAKE EXPLOSIVE BY AN UNDERCOVER FBI AGENT. HE WAS 17 YEARS OLD.[161]

ALSO PEOPLE ARRESTED FOR TWEETING "SUPPORT," LIKE 17 YEAR OLD ALI SHUKRI AMIN, WHO WAS SENTENCED TO 11 YEARS FOR HIS TWEETS AND INSTRUCTIONS ON HOW TO USE BITCOIN...[162]

ARRESTED FOR TWEETS — IN THE NAME OF PROTECTING THE U.S., THE FIRST AMENDMENT MUST NOT APPLY...

AND FINALLY, THE TARGETED DRONE KILLING OF AMERICAN CITIZEN ANWAR AL-AWLAKI, & HIS 16 YEAR OLD SON, WHO WAS ALSO AMERICAN. SO DOMESTIC POLICY IS OFTEN AS CHILLING AS THE SUPPORT OF UNDEMOCRATIC REGIMES.[163]

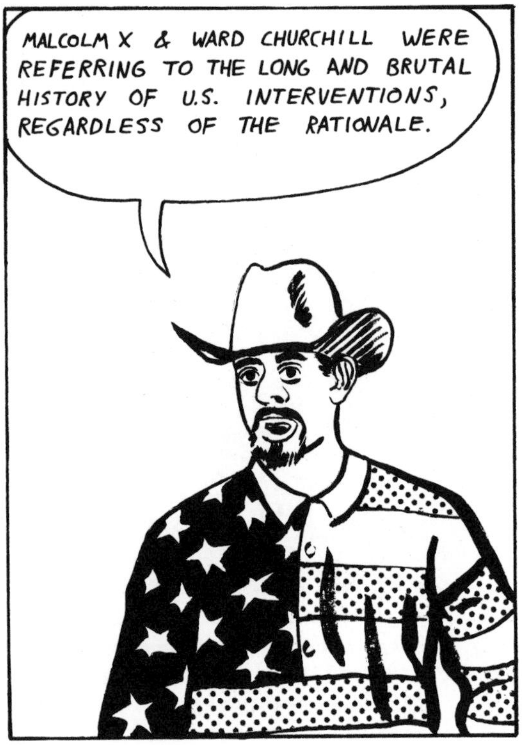
MALCOLM X & WARD CHURCHILL WERE REFERRING TO THE LONG AND BRUTAL HISTORY OF U.S. INTERVENTIONS, REGARDLESS OF THE RATIONALE.

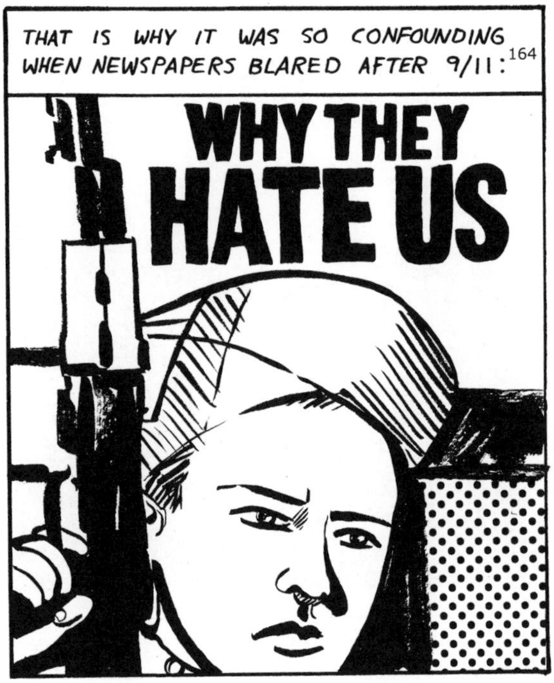
THAT IS WHY IT WAS SO CONFOUNDING WHEN NEWSPAPERS BLARED AFTER 9/11:[164]
WHY THEY HATE US

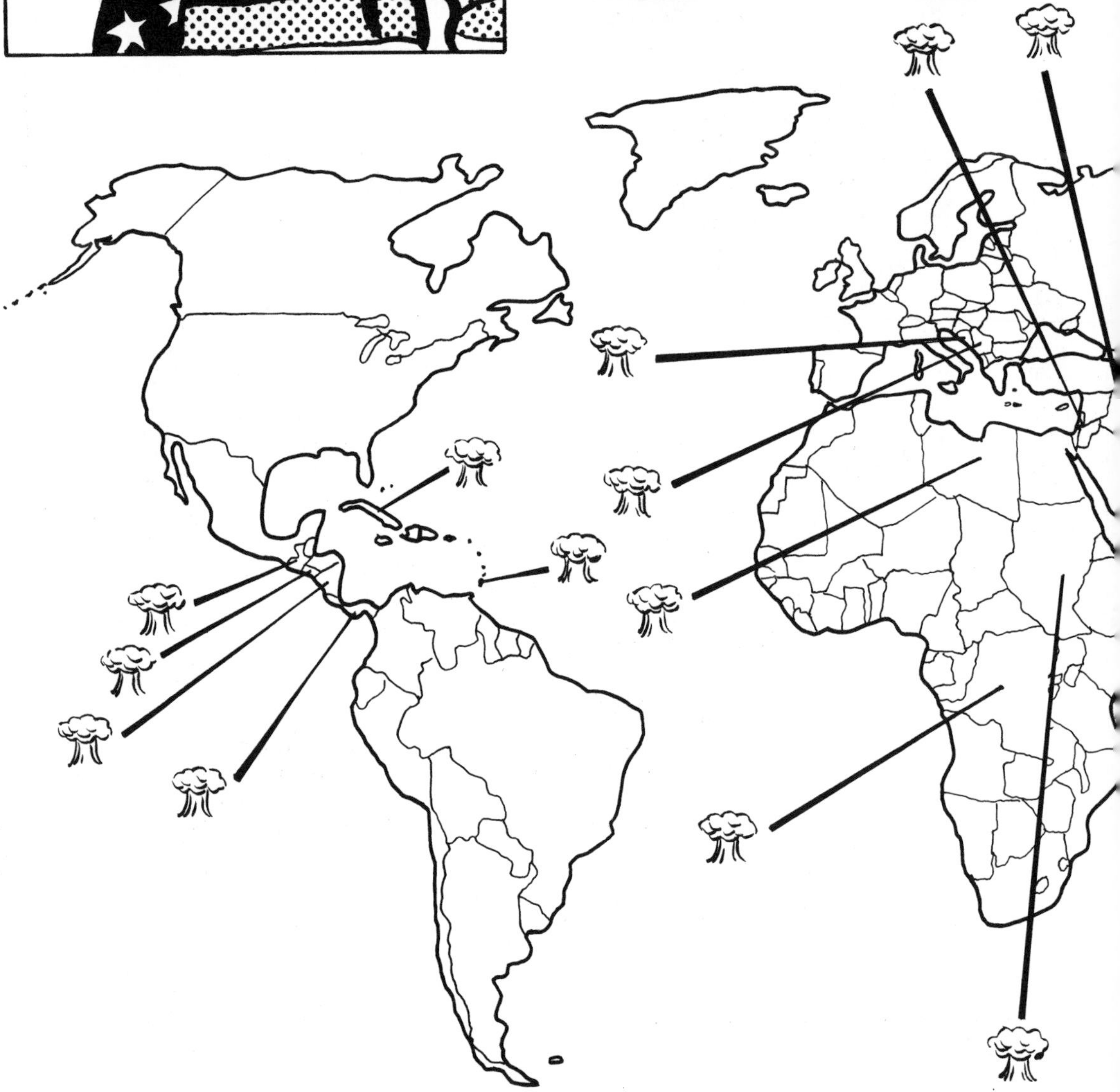

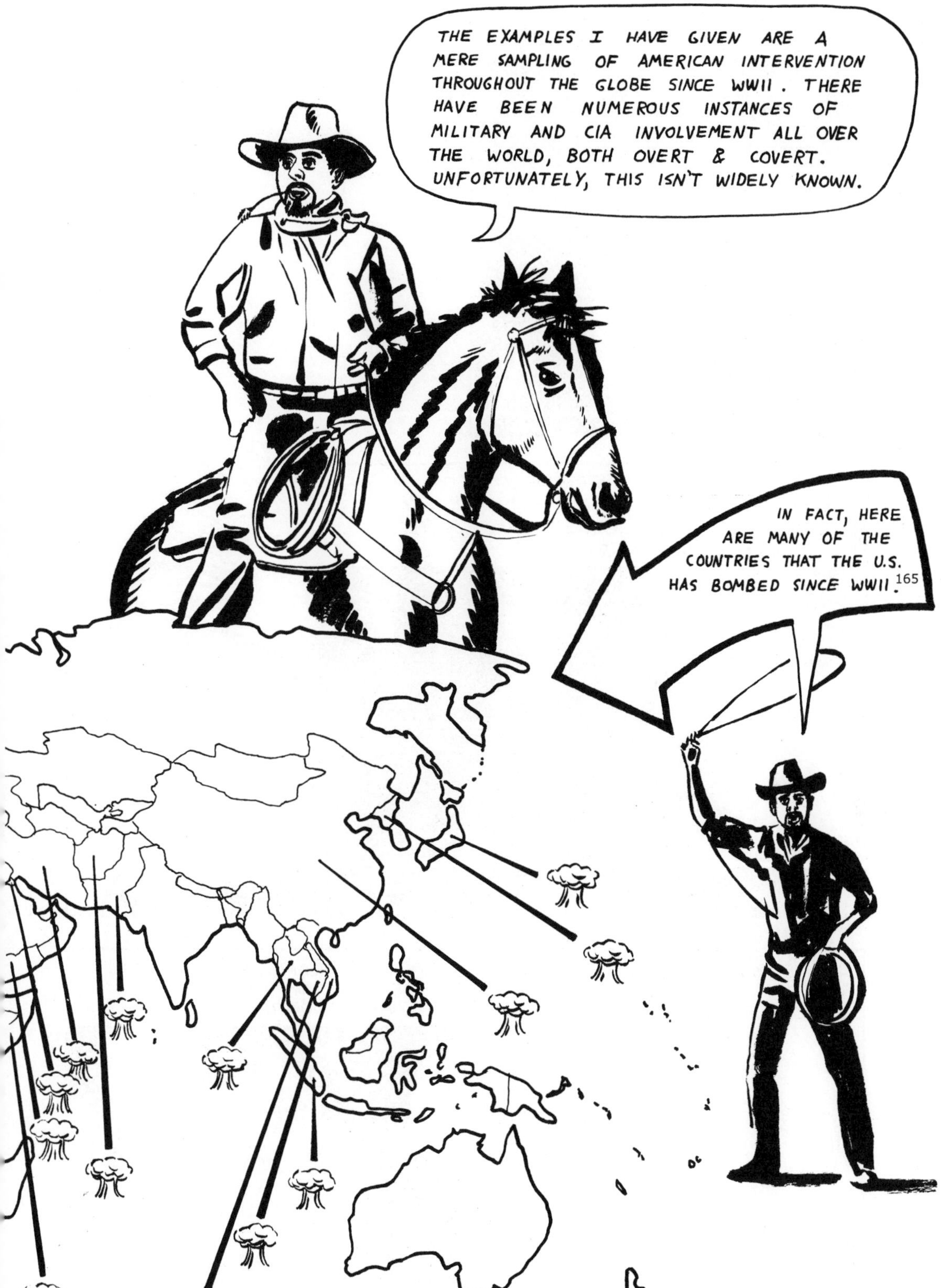
THE EXAMPLES I HAVE GIVEN ARE A MERE SAMPLING OF AMERICAN INTERVENTION THROUGHOUT THE GLOBE SINCE WWII. THERE HAVE BEEN NUMEROUS INSTANCES OF MILITARY AND CIA INVOLVEMENT ALL OVER THE WORLD, BOTH OVERT & COVERT. UNFORTUNATELY, THIS ISN'T WIDELY KNOWN.
IN FACT, HERE ARE MANY OF THE COUNTRIES THAT THE U.S. HAS BOMBED SINCE WWII.[165]

J.W. VON GOETHE ONCE SAID:

A GREAT REVOLUTION IS NEVER THE FAULT OF THE PEOPLE, BUT OF THE GOVERNMENT.[166]

BY THE END OF THE 1970s, THE SHAH OF IRAN'S POWER SEEMED ENTRENCHED BUT WITH THE ELECTION OF JIMMY CARTER CAME A PLEDGE TO EMPHASIZE "HUMAN RIGHTS."

BUT HE PUT THOSE CONCERNS TO REST ON NEW YEAR'S EVE 1977:

IRAN IS AN ISLAND OF STABILITY IN ONE OF THE MORE TROUBLED AREAS OF THE WORLD.[167]

IRONICALLY, CARTER'S STATEMENTS CAME ON THE EVE OF THE IRANIAN REVOLUTION.

STILL REELING FROM THE REVOLUTION, IRAN WAS CHAOTIC, AND THE U.S. WANTED TO PREVENT THE AYATOLLAH'S REVOLUTION FROM SPREADING.

THEN, IN 1979, YOUNG IRANIAN RADICALS TOOK OVER THE AMERICAN EMBASSY IN TEHRAN & HELD 66 AMERICANS FOR 444 DAYS.[168]

THEY UNCOVERED ILLEGAL SPYING BY THE CIA, WHICH WAS CARRIED OUT FROM INSIDE THE EMBASSY.[169]

THE RADICALS DEMANDED THE RETURN OF THE SHAH WHO FLED.

EVENTUALLY, HE WOULD DIE OF CANCER, & THE U.S. WOULD COME TO TERMS WITH IRAN. IT ALL HELPED BRING JIMMY CARTER'S PRESIDENCY TO AN END...

USHERING IN THE "REAGAN REVOLUTION" THE REAGAN CAMPAIGN CONSPIRED TO DELAY THE RELEASE OF THE AMERICANS TO HELP REAGAN'S CHANCES.[170]

IRAQ'S RULER, SADDAM HUSSEIN, TRIED TO TAKE ADVANTAGE OF THE SITUATION. WITH AMERICAN BACKING, HE WENT TO WAR WITH IRAN SEEKING TO SEIZE TERRITORY IN THE SOUTH.

HE TORE UP THE ALGIERS AGREEMENT SYMBOLICALLY ON TV AT THE START OF THE WAR.[173]

IT WAS A DISASTER FOR BOTH SIDES. ESTIMATES RANGE FROM 500,000 TO A MILLION CASUALTIES.[174]

THE U.S. KNEW IRAQ WAS LAUNCHING SOME OF THE WORST CHEMICAL ATTACKS EVER, AND THEY STILL GAVE LOGISTICAL AND OTHER SUPPORT.[175, 176]

THE U.S. SUPPORTED IRAQ, THEN IRAN.

THEY EMPLOYED THEIR CYNICAL NO WIN STRATEGY AGAIN.

WE DON'T HAVE A DOG IN THAT FIGHT.

THE WAR ENDED IN A STALEMATE. NEITHER SIDE GAINED ANYTHING.

AS THE WAR ENDED IN IRAQ AND IRAN, THE USSR WAS DEFEATED IN AFGHANISTAN.

THE ISLAMISTS CLAIMED VICTORY, AND THE TALIBAN EVENTUALLY TOOK OVER THE COUNTRY AS THE U.S. ENDED ITS INVOLVEMENT.

THE FIGHTERS BROUGHT DOWN:

THE EVIL EMPIRE.

WITH AMERICAN HELP.

THEN SADDAM HUSSEIN DID SOMETHING STUPID: HE INVADED KUWAIT.

THE COLLAPSE OF THE SOVIET UNION IN 1991 WAS ALMOST UNPRECEDENTED. THIS WOULD CHANGE THE COURSE OF POLICY FOR THE U.S. IN THE MIDDLE EAST.

MANY THOUGHT THIS NEW ERA WOULD BE A "PAX AMERICANA" - A PERIOD OF PEACE.

OF COURSE, THEY WERE WRONG...

THIS WAS SEEN AS AN OPPORTUNITY TO UNLEASH THE VISION OF AN AMERICAN DOMINATED WORLD WHILE THERE WAS NO RIVAL IN THE WAY.

GEORGE H.W. BUSH TOOK FULL ADVANTAGE OF THE NEW FREEDOM TO SECURE THE MIDDLE EAST, AND SENT TROOPS TO SAUDI ARABIA.

WHICH ANGERED OSAMA BIN LADEN WHO JUST FINISHED DISPENSING WITH THE OTHER COLD WAR POWER.

SADDAM MET WITH AMBASSADOR APRIL GLASPIE BEFORE THE INVASION OF KUWAIT. HE MAY HAVE THOUGHT THAT THE U.S. GAVE HIM A GREEN LIGHT WHEN GLASPIE SAID:[177]

WE HAVE NO OPINION ON THE ARAB — ARAB CONFLICTS, LIKE YOUR BORDER DISAGREMENT WITH KUWAIT.

IRAQ RAN UP A HUGE DEBT DURING THE IRAN/IRAQ WAR, AND THE KUWAITIS REFUSED TO FORGIVE THE DEBT.[178]

KUWAIT WAS ALSO OVERPRODUCING THEIR OIL QUOTA.[179] AND SADDAM ACCUSED THEM OF SLANT DRILLING INTO A WELL THAT STRADDLED THE BORDER BETWEEN THE COUNTRIES.[180]

IT'S DOUBTFUL SADDAM EXPECTED THE U.S. RESPONSE. WHO COULD BLAME HIM? THE U.S. WAS HIS ALLY.

I HEARD A JOKE ONCE:

THE UNITED STATES DROPPED ALL THE BOMBS IT WAS SAVING UP FOR THE SOVIET UNION ON IRAQ.

OVER ABOUT 40 DAYS AND NIGHTS THEY UNLEASHED ONE OF THE MOST SUSTAINED BOMBING CAMPAIGNS IN HISTORY.[181]

THEY DROPPED MORE BOMBS ON IRAQ THAN ALL THE BOMBS DROPPED DURING WORLD WAR II.[182]

CIVILIAN INFRASTRUCTURE LIKE, WATER TREATMENT PLANTS, THE ELECTRICAL GRID, AND OTHER NON-MILITARY TARGETS, WERE HIT.[183]

THOUSANDS OF CIVILIANS WERE KILLED OR DISPLACED.[184]

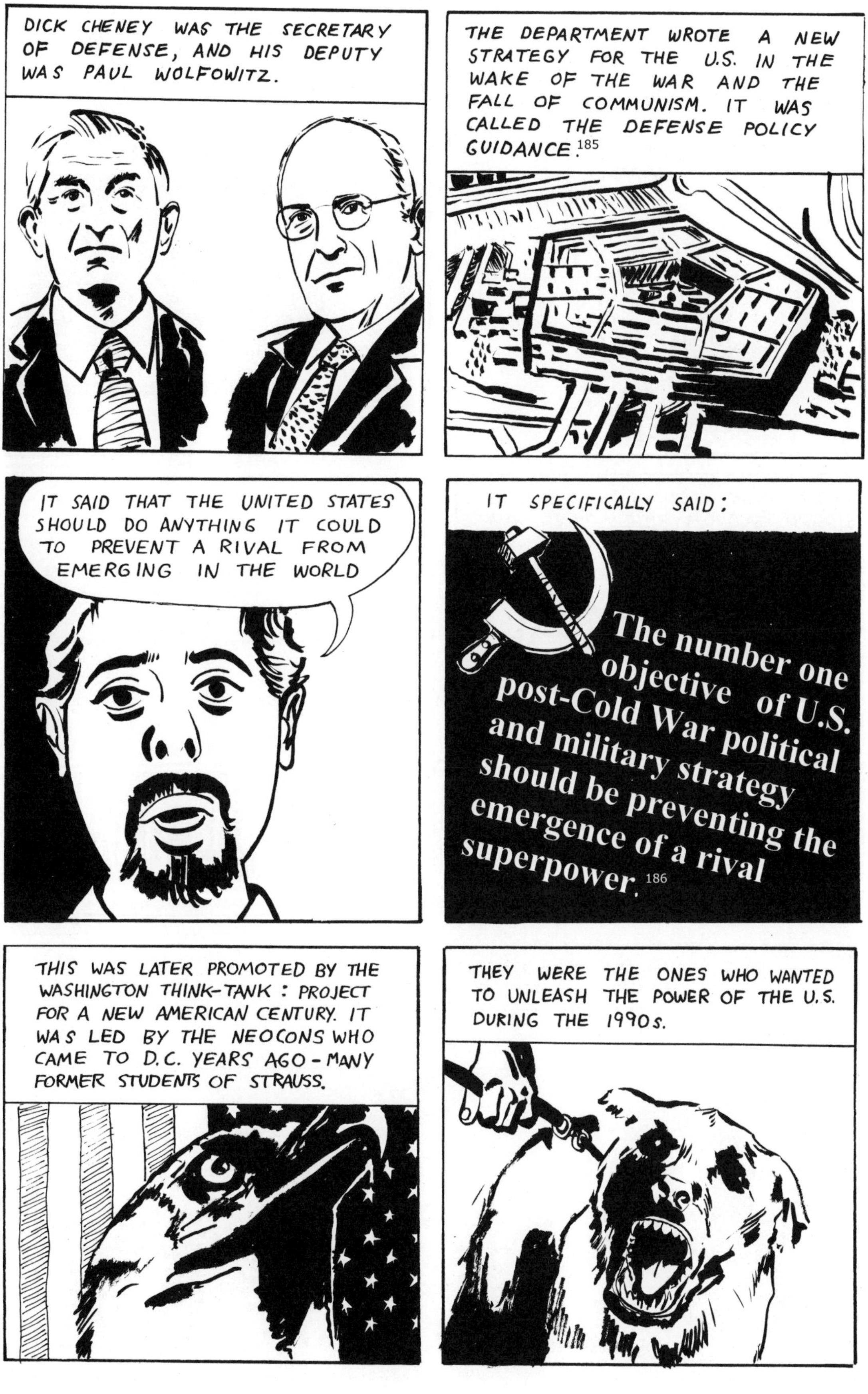
DICK CHENEY WAS THE SECRETARY OF DEFENSE, AND HIS DEPUTY WAS PAUL WOLFOWITZ.
THE DEPARTMENT WROTE A NEW STRATEGY FOR THE U.S. IN THE WAKE OF THE WAR AND THE FALL OF COMMUNISM. IT WAS CALLED THE DEFENSE POLICY GUIDANCE.[185]
IT SAID THAT THE UNITED STATES SHOULD DO ANYTHING IT COULD TO PREVENT A RIVAL FROM EMERGING IN THE WORLD
IT SPECIFICALLY SAID:
The number one objective of U.S. post-Cold War political and military strategy should be preventing the emergence of a rival superpower.[186]
THIS WAS LATER PROMOTED BY THE WASHINGTON THINK-TANK : PROJECT FOR A NEW AMERICAN CENTURY. IT WAS LED BY THE NEOCONS WHO CAME TO D.C. YEARS AGO - MANY FORMER STUDENTS OF STRAUSS.
THEY WERE THE ONES WHO WANTED TO UNLEASH THE POWER OF THE U.S. DURING THE 1990s.

THE IDEA WAS TO SECURE ACCESS TO OIL—AND THE ABILITY TO CONTROL THE FLOW—IF THERE WAS EVER A SERIOUS REASON TO DO THAT.

IN THIS WAY, THEY WOULD HAVE POTENTIAL POWER OVER FOES. CHINA HAS BECOME AMERICA'S ECONOMIC RIVAL, SURPASSING JAPAN AS THE WORLD'S SECOND LARGEST ECONOMY.[187]

AFTER JAPAN, GERMANY IS THE 4TH BIGGEST ECONOMY—THEY DON'T HAVE LARGE OIL RESOURCES.

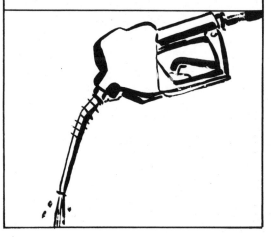

THESE NATIONS ARE PART OF A WORLD COMPETITION TO SECURE ACCESS TO THIS RESOURCE, WHICH IS VITAL TO ECONOMIES.

IN FACT, CHINA IS INDUSTRIALIZING AT A BREAKNECK SPEED AND WILL EVENTUALLY PASS THE U.S.—CHINA USED MORE CONCRETE IN 3 YEARS (2011–13) THAN THE U.S. USED IN 100 YEARS (1900–2000).[188]

BACK IN 1991, BILL CLINTON WAS ELECTED, BUT HE WASN'T A NEOCON.

THE IDEA WAS TO HAVE THE MOST POWERFUL MILITARY IN THE HEART OF THE ENERGY PRODUCING WORLD (IN SAUDI ARABIA), WHICH HAS ISLAM'S HOLIEST PLACE.

SO RIGHT-WINGERS WANTED TO REMOVE ANY OBSTACLE TO AMERICAN DOMINANCE.

EVEN THOUGH SADDAM'S ARMY WAS DECIMATED — HE WAS LEFT IN POWER.

INDEED, THE U.S. OBLITERATED RETREATING IRAQI FORCES ON THE ROAD FROM KUWAIT BACK TO IRAQ. THOUSANDS WERE KILLED BY AIRCRAFT IN WHAT BECAME KNOWN AS "THE HIGHWAY OF DEATH." [189]

AMERICAN PRESS REFUSED TO PUBLISH A PHOTO TAKEN BY KENNETH JARECKE SHOWING AN IRAQI SOLDIER BURNED ALIVE IN HIS VEHICLE. [190]

107

SO, SADDAM WAS STILL THERE — A THORN IN THE SIDE OF U.S. POWER. CLINTON CARED MORE ABOUT DOMESTIC AFFAIRS, & BECAME EMBROILED IN HIS OWN EMBARRASSMENTS.

THAT DIDN'T STOP CLINTON FROM ATTACKING IRAQ IN 1998 WITH "OPERATION DESERT FOX," WHICH BOMBED MANY SITES, INCLUDING A BABY MILK FACTORY.[191]

THE PRETEXT FOR BOMBING WAS THAT SADDAM WASN'T COOPERATING WITH UN WEAPONS INSPECTORS. MANY SAW IT AS A "WAG THE DOG" SENARIO.[192]

WAG THE DOG

SECRETARY OF THE JOINT CHIEFS OF STAFF HUGH SHELTON (UNDER CLINTON) WAS ASKED IF IT WAS POSSIBLE TO ENGINEER A U.S. WARPLANE BEING SHOT DOWN BY IRAQ SO THE INCIDENT COULD BE USED AS AN EXCUSE FOR BOMBING.[193] SHELTON CALLED THE LEAD UP TO THE 2003 IRAQ INVASION:

DECEPTION AND LIES.[194]

CLINTON ALSO MAINTAINED ECONOMIC SANCTIONS AGAINST IRAQ, WHICH DECIMATED THE WEAKEST OF ITS POPULATION.

WHEN ASKED IF THE SANCTIONS-RELATED DEATHS OF 500,000 CHILDREN WAS WORTH IT, SECRETARY OF STATE MADELINE ALBRIGHT SAID:

IT'S A HARD CHOICE BUT, YES, WE THINK IT'S WORTH IT.[195]

THE BIGGEST HEALTH PROBLEM FOR IRAQI CHILDREN BEFORE THE WAR WAS OBESITY. AFTER THE WAR, IT BECAME MALNUTRITION & PREVENTABLE DISEASE...

ALL AS A RESULT OF THE DESTRUCTION OF THE CIVILIAN INFRASTRUCTURE, & SANCTIONS THAT PREVENTED MEDICINE & BASIC GOODS FROM ENTERING THE COUNTRY DURING THE 1990s.

THE SANCTIONS WERE SO BARBARIC THAT UN ASSISTANT SECRETARY GENERAL, DENIS HALLIDAY, RESIGNED IN PROTEST.[196]

ALL THIS HAPPENED BEFORE GEORGE W. BUSH WAS ELECTED.

AFTER 9/11, THE NEOCONS WERE ALREADY IN HIS CABINET, AND THEY WENT INTO ACTION.

ALL FANTASIES AND MYTHS THAT STRAUSS WOULD HAVE BEEN PROUD OF.

AND ON THE OTHER SIDE: THE FUNDAMENTALISTS, WHO SAW THE INVASIONS OF AFGHANISTAN AND IRAQ AS PART OF THEIR HOLY WAR, LIKE THE WAR AGAINST THE GODLESS SOVIET UNION.

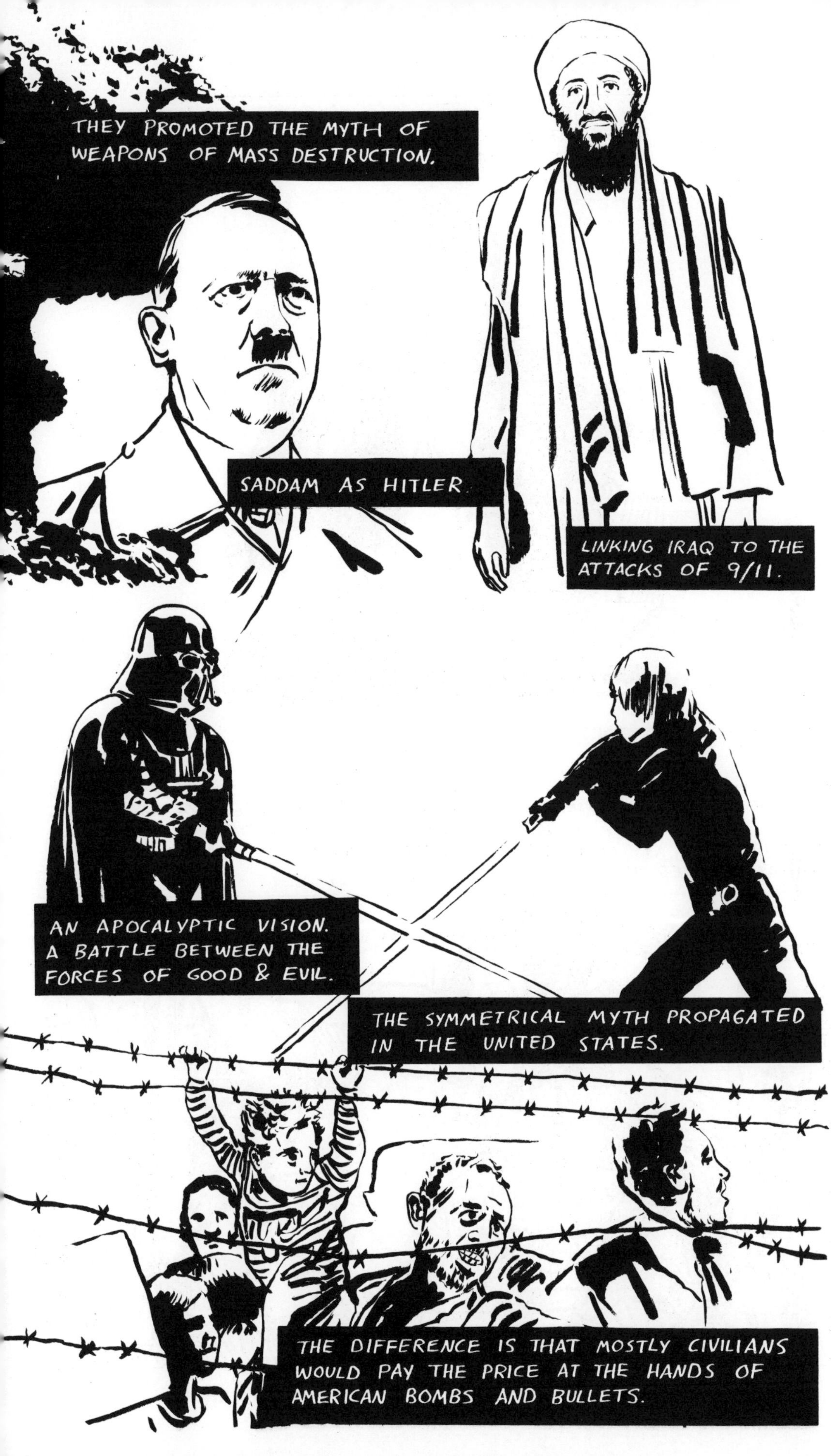
THEY PROMOTED THE MYTH OF WEAPONS OF MASS DESTRUCTION.
SADDAM AS HITLER.
LINKING IRAQ TO THE ATTACKS OF 9/11.
AN APOCALYPTIC VISION. A BATTLE BETWEEN THE FORCES OF GOOD & EVIL.
THE SYMMETRICAL MYTH PROPAGATED IN THE UNITED STATES.
THE DIFFERENCE IS THAT MOSTLY CIVILIANS WOULD PAY THE PRICE AT THE HANDS OF AMERICAN BOMBS AND BULLETS.

IN MAKING THE CASE FOR WAR AT THE UNITED NATIONS, COLIN POWELL DESCRIBED HOW JUST A SMALL VIAL OF ANTHRAX COULD KILL THOUSANDS.

ONE OF PICASSO'S MASTERPIECES, GUERNICA, IS ON DISPLAY AT UNITED NATIONS HEADQUARTERS. IT DEPICTS THE SAVAGE, INDISCRIMINATE, BOMBING OF THE TOWN OF GUERNICA BY FASCISTS DURING THE SPANISH CIVIL WAR. IT WAS COVERED UP.[197]

112

THE DISASTROUS 2003 WAR IN IRAQ LED TO MANY UNINTENDED CONSEQUENCES. THE RULE OF L. PAUL BREMMER WAS A FIASCO. HE DISBANDED THE IRAQI ARMY, LEAVING MANY MEN WITHOUT INCOME OR OCCUPATION. MANY OF THOSE SOLDIERS & OFFICERS BECAME LEADERS IN THE ISLAMIC STATE.

THE RISE OF ISIS WAS A LOGICAL OUTCOME. IN A WAR THAT HAS SEEN MUCH RUTHLESS BRUTALITY, IT STANDS TO REASON THAT THE MOST VIOLENT WILL MAKE ADVANCES.

THEY ARE THE OFFSPRING OF AL QAEDA, THE DESCENDANTS OF SAID QUTB, & THE LEGACY OF U.S. INTERVENTION IN THE REGION.

EVEN THOUGH OBAMA WITHDREW MOST TROOPS IN 2011, THE U.S. IS STILL INTERVENING IN THE REGION.

DIPLOMAT LAKHDAR BRAHIMI SAID:

NO DOUBT THAT THE ORIGINAL SIN WHICH LED TO THE EMERGENCE OF ISIS IS THE U.S. — LED INVASION OF IRAQ. THERE WAS NO JUSTIFICATION FOR THE WAR IN IRAQ, AND WE ALL SUFFER THE CONSEQUENCES.[198]

THE FORCES OF CHANGE ARE SWEEPING THROUGH THE REGION, BRINGING VIOLENCE, INSTABILITY, AND THE HOPE FOR FREEDOM. THIS BEGAN IN TUNISIA IN 2011, AND IN EGYPT IN 2011, AND CONTINUES IN OTHER COUNTRIES.

THIS HAS ALSO RESULTED IN THE CIVIL WARS IN SYRIA & IRAQ, CAUSING A HUGE REFUGEE CRISIS.

IT'S HARD TO KNOW WHAT THE FUTURE HOLDS. IT'S TRUE THAT REVOLUTIONARIES MAKE THEIR OWN HISTORY, AS KARL MARX ONCE PUT IT:

THEY DO NOT MAKE IT JUST AS THEY PLEASE; THEY DO NOT MAKE IT UNDER CIRCUMSTANCES CHOSEN BY THEMSELVES, BUT UNDER CIRCUMSTANCES DIRECTLY ENCOUNTERED AND TRANSMITTED FROM THE PAST.

JOSEPH MASSAD SAID THAT:

GUARDING AGAINST THE CO-OPTATION OF THE TUNISIAN AND EGYPTIAN REVOLUTIONS IS THE HOPE OF ALL ARABS.[199]

BUT THE U.S. STILL SUPPORTS CORRUPT REGIMES LIKE:

THE ABSOLUTE MONARCHY OF SAUDI ARABIA (WHICH IS SUPPRESSING OR MILITARILY CHALLENGING DEMOCRATIC MOVEMENTS)...

AND THE OTHER GULF MONARCHIES...

THE GOVERNMENT OF ISRAEL...

AND THE AFGHAN REGIME — THE VICE PRESIDENT, AHMED ZIA MASSOUD, VISITED THE UNITED ARAB EMIRATES WHERE AUTHORITES, WORKING WITH THE DRUG ENFORCEMENT ADMINISTRATION, DISCOVERED HE WAS CARRYING 52 MILLION DOLLARS IN CASH.

HE WAS ALLOWED TO KEEP IT. [200]

TODAY, THE U.S. AGENCY FOR INTERNATIONAL DEVELOPMENT AND STATE DEPARTMENT (COMPRISING 2,000 & 30,000 EMPLOYEES RESPECTIVELY) SHARE A $50 BILLION FOREIGN AFFAIRS BUDGET...[201]

WHILE THE PENTAGON MAINTAINS MORE THAN 1.6 MILLION EMPLOYEES AND A BUDGET UPWARDS OF $600 BILLION.[202]

LIKE THEY SAY, TO A MAN WITH A HAMMER, EVERYTHING LOOKS LIKE A NAIL.

THE UNITED STATES IS THE LARGEST SPENDER ON ITS MILITARY BUDGET IN THE ENTIRE WORLD. THE UNITED STATES SPENDS AT LEAST AS MUCH ON ITS MILITARY AS THE NEXT 10 COUNTRIES IN THE WORLD COMBINED.[203]

GULF PETRODOLLARS ARE RECYCLED BACK INTO THE U.S. ECONOMY. THE U.S. BUYS OIL, AND MANY OF THOSE MONARCHIES USE ALOA LOT THAT MONEY TO BUY EXPENSIVE WEAPONS.

SAUDI ARABIA, A CLOSE ALLY OF THE U.S.A, SPENDS BILLIONS A YEAR ON ITS MILITARY. IT RECENTLY BECAME THE 3RD BIGGEST SPENDER IN THE WORLD.[204]

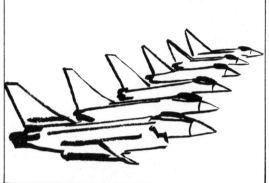

WHILE AMERICA GIVES ISRAEL ABOUT 3 BILLION DOLLARS IN AID AND ARMS A YEAR.[205]

ISRAEL USES THIS AID TO SETTLE PALESTINIAN LAND, AND USES THESE SOPHISTICATED WEAPONS ON A CIVILIAN POPULATION (NOT ONLY TO KILL BUT TO ALSO CAUSE TERROR). THEY USE U.S. SUPPLIED FIGHTER JETS OVER RESIDENTIAL AREAS TO CREATE SONIC BOOMS. THIS PRACTICE HAS GIVEN CHILDREN HEARING PROBLEMS AND PSYCHOLOGICAL DISORDERS.[206]

ISRAEL (AND THE U.S.) ALSO USES WHITE PHOSPHORUS AND CLUSTER BOMBS.

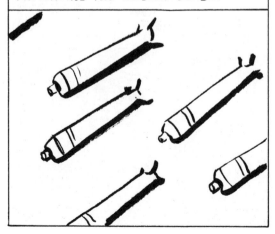

CLUSTER BOMBS EXPLODE OVER AREAS & SPREAD HUNDREDS OF "BOMBLETS" THAT ARE PACKED WITH SHRAPNEL. THEY ARE INDISCRIMINATE.

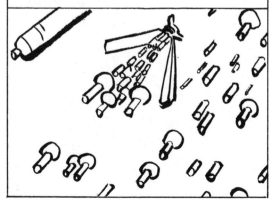

AND YET, THE MILITARY SPENDING CONTINUES & INCREASES. OBAMA IS RESPONSIBLE FOR THE BIGGEST MILITARY BUDGET SINCE WWII.[207]

PEOPLE WERE OFFERED OPTIMISTIC AGENDAS FOR A BETTER WORLD. THE HEIGHT OF THIS IDEALISM WAS THE 1960s AS MOVEMENTS FLOURISHED THROUGHOUT THE WORLD.

FRANCE

MEXICO

HASTA LA VICTOR

USA

CHINA

THE PROMISE OF THIS ERA FADED, AND MANY TURNED TO NEW IDEOLOGIES. OTHERS HAVE ARGUED THAT WE HAVE ENTERED AN AGE OF DISILLUSION. TERROR IS ARGUABLEY THE ULTIMATE MOTIVATOR – POSSIBLY MORE THAN THE IDEALISM OF THE PAST...

SHAKESPEARE WROTE,

TO-MORROW, AND TO-MORROW, AND TO-MORROW,

CREEPS IN THIS PETTY PACE FROM DAY TO DAY,

TO THE LAST SYLLABLE OF RECORDED TIME,

AND ALL OUR YESTERDAYS HAVE LIGHTED FOOLS THE WAY TO DUSTY DEATH.

OUT, OUT, BRIEF CANDLE!

LIFE'S BUT A WALKING SHADOW, A POOR PLAYER, THAT STRUTS AND FRETS HIS HOUR UPON THE STAGE, AND THEN IS HEARD NO MORE.

IT IS A TALE TOLD BY AN IDIOT, FULL OF SOUND AND FURY,

SIGNIFYING NOTHING.[208]

THE LEADERS OF BOTH SIDES OF "THE WAR ON TERROR" HAVE SEIZED ON OUR AGE OF DISILLUSIONMENT IN POLITICS.

HANNAH ARENDT ONCE SAID:

THE MOST RADICAL REVOLUTIONARY WILL BECOME A CONSERVATIVE THE DAY AFTER THE REVOLUTION.[209, 210]

BEFORE, PEOPLE WERE MOBILIZED FOR "GREAT CAUSES."

BUT TODAY, MANY PEOPLE HAVE LOST FAITH IN POLITICS.

REGIMES RULE BY CONSENT, FORCE, OR A COMBINATION OF THE TWO. IN AMERICA, WE HAVE AN ILLUSION OF CONSENT, BASED ON CORPORATE MEDIA NARRATIVE, CONSUMERISM, AND FEAR.

FEAR, RELIGION, ACTUAL GRIEVANCES, ALL THESE THINGS ARE FODDER FOR THE PURSUIT OF POWER. BUT THE MOST IMPORTANT QUESTION TO ASK IS: IN WHOSE INTERESTS DOES THAT POWER SERVE?

DESPITE THE RISE OF ISIS...

AND THE UNITED STATES' RECKLESS MILITARY ACTIONS, WHICH HAVE COST THE LIVES OF THOUSANDS OF CIVILIANS.

OBAMA'S ATTACKS AGAINST ISIS ALONE HAVE RESULTED IN THE DEATHS OF AT LEAST 459 CIVILIANS SINCE 2014.[211]

DESPITE MASS SHOOTINGS IN THE U.S. AND EUROPE, WE LIVE IN A RELATIVLEY PEACEFUL PERIOD.[212]

THERE ARE MANY REASONS FOR PESSIMISM BUT OUR FEARS ARE OFTEN STOKED BY THOSE SEEKING POWER.

WORLDWIDE, MORE PEOPLE DIE FROM DOMESTIC HOMICIDES THAN FROM TERRORISM OR WAR. WHY CAN FEAR RULE US?[213]

FEAR IS YOUR ONLY GOD.

THE RISE OF DONALD TRUMP IS EMBLEMATIC OF THIS LOSS OF FAITH.

THE GLOBAL FORCES OF CAPITAL HAVE CREATED ECONOMIC ANXIETY.

POPULATION DISPLACEMENT.

WAR AND CONCENTRATION OF WEALTH AND POWER.

AND THE LIBERALS OF THE UNITED STATES HAVE HISTORICALLY KEPT THE STATUS QUO (WITH SOME EXCEPTIONS).

TRUMP'S "ANTI-POLITICS" IS VERY APPEALING TO A DISAFFECTED PUBLIC.

MAYBE WE ARE ALL NIHILISTS NOW?
MAYBE WE SEE THE HORROR AND WANT
TO RETREAT FROM IT?

INTRACTABLE CONFLICT...

WORLD POVERTY...

UNSTOPPABLE CLIMATE CHANGE...

DECEITFUL LEADERS...

WAS EVIL MORE CLEARLY DEFINED IN
THE PAST? MAYBE STRAUSS WAS RIGHT,
DO WE NEED A LIE?

Epilogue...

الخاتمه...

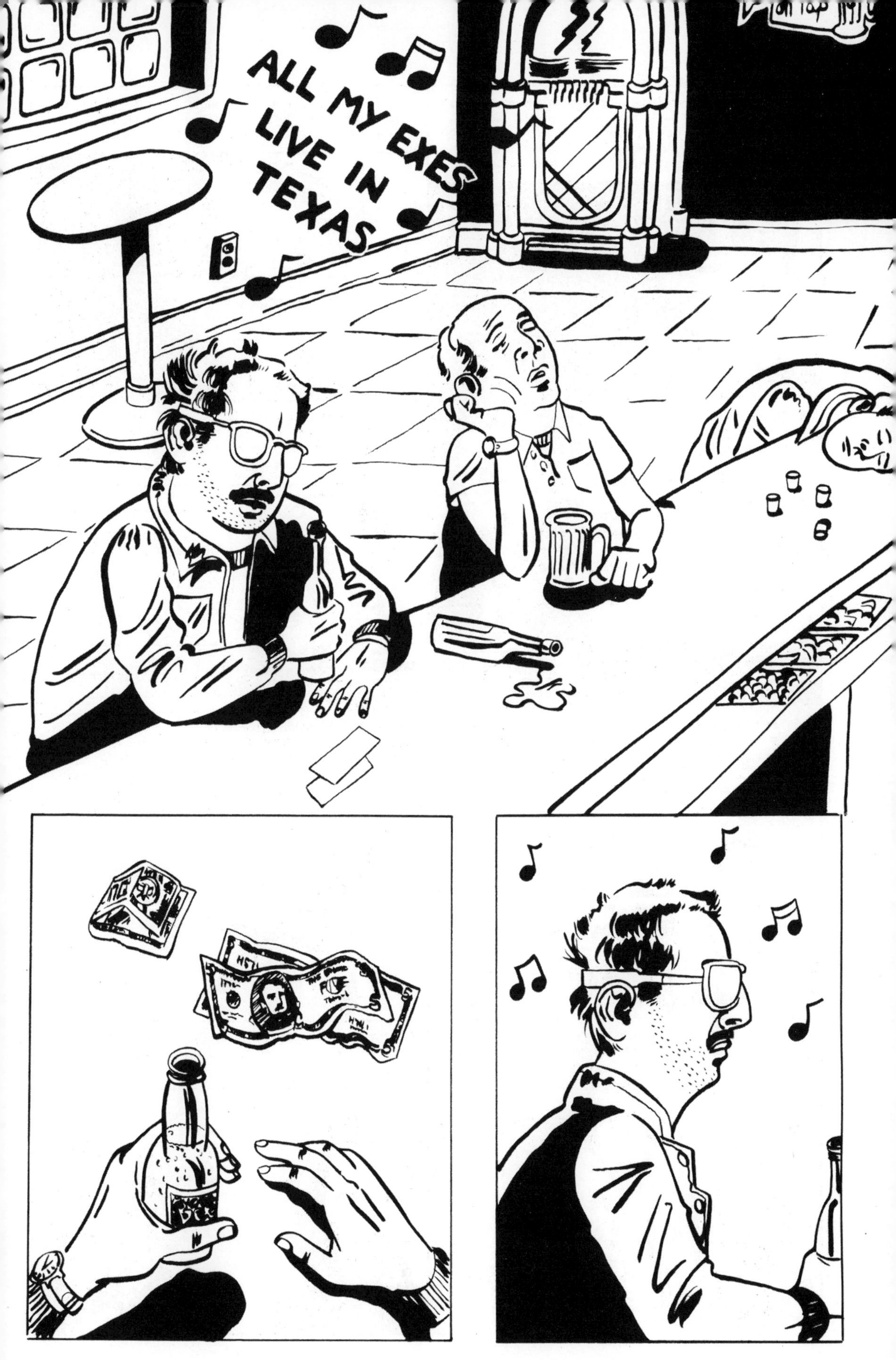
ALL MY EXES LIVE IN TEXAS

EIGHT YEARS AGO PEOPLE CELEBRATED THE FIRST BLACK PRESIDENT OF THE USA. MANY HOPED THAT AMERICA WOULD FINALLY RECKON WITH ITS PAST AND START TO MOVE PAST ITS HISTORY OF RAPACIOUS CAPITALISM, IMPERIALISM AND RACISM.

WITH THE ELECTION OF TRUMP, IT IS HARD TO BELIEVE THAT ANYONE EVER HAD HOPE FOR A CHANGE IN THE CHARACTER OF THE USA.

CORNEL WEST SAID:

IT COULD EASILY PRODUCE A PERVASIVE CYNICISM AND POISONOUS NIHILISM. IS THERE REALLY ANY HOPE FOR TRUTH AND JUSTICE IN THIS DECADENT TIME? DOES AMERICA EVEN HAVE THE CAPACITY TO BE HONEST ABOUT ITSELF AND COME TO TERMS WITH ITS SELF-DESTRUCTIVE ADDICTION TO MONEY-WORSHIP AND COWARDLY XENOPHOBIA?[214]

OBAMA WAS NEVER HELD TO ACCOUNT, AND THIS HELPED PAVE THE WAY FOR THE CURRENT SITUATION. LISTENING TO HIS NEOLIBERAL ADVISERS, IN 2009 HE MET WITH WALL STREET LEADERS. HE TOLD THEM:

MY ADMINISTRATION IS THE ONLY THING BETWEEN YOU AND THE PITCHFORKS.[215]

NOT ONE WALL STREET EXECUTIVE WENT TO JAIL.

ON OBAMA'S WATCH, ISRAELI DEFENSE FORCES KILLED MORE THAN 2,000 PALESTINIANS (INCLUDING 550 CHILDREN) IN 50 DAYS. HE GAVE AN ADDITIONAL 225 MILLION DOLLARS TO THE ISRAELI MILITARY.

IN FACT, THE NOBEL PEACE PRIZE WINNING OBAMA DROPPED 26,171 BOMBS IN 2016 ALONE.. SO, IN JUST ONE YEAR, THE U.S. DROPPED 72 BOMBS A DAY, 3 BOMBS EVERY HOUR, 24 HOURS A DAY. MOST BOMBS FELL ON MUSLIM MAJORITY COUNTRIES.[216]

IN JULY 2016 THE U.S. ABSURDLY CLAIMED IT KILLED ONLY 116 CIVILIANS IN PAKISTAN, YEMEN, SOMALIA AND LIBYA FROM 2009 TO 2015. THE BUREAU OF INVESTIGATIVE JOURNALISM SAYS THE TRUE FIGURE IS SIX TIMES HIGHER.[217]

OBAMA COULD HAVE CONFRONTED NEOLIBERALISM, BUT HE DIDN'T. RALPH WALDO EMERSON AND HERMAN MELVILLE HAVE BOTH SAID:

SOW A CHARACTER AND YOU REAP A DESTINY.

THE CLAIMS THAT THE WAR IN IRAQ WAS NOT ABOUT OIL HAVE PROVED FALSE. 15 YEARS LATER MANY OF THE ARCHITECTS OF THE WAR ARE CASHING IN. BRITISH PETROLEUM STARTED OPERATING THE RUMAILIA OIL FIELD IN 2009. IT IS ONE OF THE BIGGEST FIELDS IN THE WORLD, PRODUCING 100 MILLION DOLLARS A DAY.

DURING THE OCCUPATION, THE ENTIRE YEARLY HEALTH BUDGET OF IRAQ WAS $500 MILLION.

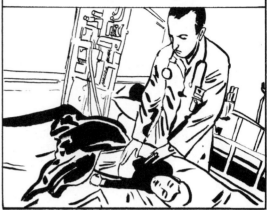

FORMER CHIEF OF BRITAIN'S MI6 SIR JOHN SAWERS WAS THE UK'S SPECIAL REPRESENTATIVE DURING THE OCCUPATION. HE LEFT MI6 IN 2014 AND IS NOW A BP "INDEPENDENT NON-EXECUTIVE DIRECTOR."

IN 2003, BP SAID IT HAD NO "STRATEGIC INTEREST" IN IRAQ, AND PRIME MINISTER TONY BLAIR SAID THAT "THE OIL CONSPIRACY" WAS:

MOST ABSURD.

BUT BP MET WITH LABOUR PEER LADY SYMONDS TO LOBBY FOR A SHARE OF THE OIL

A MEMO FROM A MEETING BETWEEN BP, SHELL, AND BG SAID: "BARONESS SYMONDS AGREED IT WOULD BE DIFFICULT TO JUSTIFY BRITISH COMPANIES LOSING OUT IN IRAQ."

MINUTES FROM ANOTHER MEETING WITH THE FOREIGN OFFICE: "BP IS DESPERATE TO GET IN THERE AND ANXIOUS THAT POLITICAL DEALS SHOULD NOT DENY THEM THE OPPORTUNITY."

IT IS JUST LIKE THE 1953 COUP IN IRAN ALL OVER AGAIN.

NOTES

1. Zenko, Micah. "America Is a Safe Place." *Politics, Power, and Preventive Action,* Council on Foreign Relations, 24 Feb. 2012, blogs.cfr.org/zenko/2012/02/24/america-is-a-safe-place/. Accessed 4 May 2016.

2. Ibid.

3. Morgado, Javier. "New Day." *New Day.* Buber, John. Cable News Network (CNN). June 2015. Television.

4. Shaikh, Nermeen and German, Mike. "Does U.S. Ignore Right-Wing Terror? More Killed by White Extremists Than Jihadists Since 9/11." Interview by Amy Goodman. *Democracy Now!,* 25 June 2015. www.democracynow.org/2015/6/25/does_us_ignore_right_wing_terror.

5. Gelling, Peter. "White Americans are the biggest terror threat in the United States." *Global Post.* Public Radio International, 24 July. 2015, www.globalpost.com/article/6592741/2015/06/24/white-americans-are-biggest-terror-threat-united-states. Accessed 12 Dec 2016.

6. Kaminsky, Jonathan. " U.S. White supremacist pleads guilty in Pacific Northwest killing spree." *Reuters*, 23 April. 2014, www.reuters.com/article/2014/04/24/us-usa-crime-supremacist-idUSBREA3N02G20140424. Accessed 12 Dec. 2016.

7. Saletan, William. "The Chattanooga Killings Aren't Terrorism." *Slate,* 17 July. 2015, www.slate.com/articles/news_and_politics/foreigners/2015/07/the_chattanooga_killings_aren_t_terrorism_they_are_a_rational_horrific_act.html. Accessed 5 Jan 2017. Accessed 12 Dec. 2016.

8. Ibid.

9. Zinn, Howard. *Terrorism and War*. Seven Stories Press, 2002.

10. Ibid.

11. Dunham, Will. "Deaths in Vietnam, other wars undercounted: study Washington." *Reuters*, 19 June. 2008, www.reuters.com/article/2008/06/19/us-war-deaths-idUSN1928547620080619. Accessed 12 Dec. 2016.

12. "BBC News Flashback: 1991 Gulf War." *BBC News,* 20 March. 2003, news.bbc.co.uk/2/hi/middle_east/2754103.stm.

13. *Iraq Body Count*. ifa (Institut für Auslandsbeziehungen) with means of the German Federal Foreign Office and The Joseph Rowntree Charitable Trust, 2003, www.iraqbodycount.org/. Accessed 12 December 2016.

14. Zenko, Micah. "Clear and Present Safety: The United States Is More Secure than Washington Thinks." *Politics, Power, and Preventive Action,* Council on Foreign Relations, 23 Feb. 2012, blogs.cfr.org/zenko/2012/02/23/clear-and-present-safety-the-united-states-is-more-secure-than-washington-thinks/. Accessed 12 Dec. 2016.

15. "Global goofs: U.S. youth can't find Iraq." *CNN Friday*, 22 November. 2002, archives.cnn.com/2002/EDUCATION/11/20/geography.quiz/.

16. Fisher, Max. " Half of Americans can't Identify Syria on a Map." *Washington Post,* 26 April 2013. www.washingtonpost.com/blogs/worldviews/wp/2013/04/26/half-of-americans-cant-identify-syria-on-a-map-young-republicans-do-slightly-better/.

17. Roach, John. "Young Americans Geographically Illiterate, Survey Suggests." *National Geographic News,* 2 May. 2006, news.nationalgeographic.com/news/2006/05/0502_060502_geography_2.html.

18. "POLL SAYS 41% OF AMERICANS BELIEVE HUMANS AND DINOSAURS COEXISTED." *Daily Kos*, 25 June. 2015, www.dailykos.com/story/2015/06/25/1396630/-Poll-says-41-of-Americans-believe-humans-and-dinosaurs-coexisted#. Accessed 17 Dec. 2016.

19. "Poll: Nearly 8 in 10 Americans believe in angels." *CBS News,* 23 December. 2011, www.cbsnews.com/news/poll-nearly-8-in-10-americans-believe-in-angels/.

20. Morford, Mark. "37 percent of people completely lost." *SFgate,* 12 March. 2013, blog.sfgate.com/morford/2013/03/12/37-percent-of-people-completely-lost/. Accessed 11 Dec. 2016.

21. Milbank, Dana and Deane, Claudia. "Hussein Link to 9/11 Lingers in Many Minds." *Washington Post*, 6 September 2003. www. washingtonpost.com/ac2/wp-dyn/A32862-2003Sep5?language=printer.

22. Neuman, Johanna. "Missing Iraq antiquities haunt experts." *Los Angeles Times,* 9 April 2008. www.latimes.com/news/nationworld/world/middleeast/la-na-antiquities9apr09,1,5355912.story.

23. *Lost Treasures*. University of Chicago: Oriental Institute, 2008, oi.uchicago.edu/OI/IRAQ/iraq.html. Accessed 3 Jan. 2017.

24. "Chasing Down History and the 'Thieves of Baghdad.'" *Morning Edition.* National Public Radio. 9 December. 2005, www.npr.org/templates/story/story.php?storyId=5024219.

25. Harms, William. " O.I. marks 5-year-old 'catastrophe' at Baghdad museum: Illicit trade in antiquities promotes looting of unprotected repositories." *The University of Chicago Chronicle*, Vol. 27, No. 13, 3 April 2008, chronicle.uchicago.edu/080403/catastrophe.shtml. Accessed 12 December 2016.

26. Abdullah, Thabit A.J. *A Short History of Iraq*. Pearson Longman, 2003.

27. Tripp, *Charles. History of Iraq*. Cambridge University Press, 2000.

28. Abdullah, Thabit A.J. *A Short History of Iraq*. Pearson Longman, 2003.

29. Wheelan, Joseph. *Jefferson's War: America's First War on Terror 1801–1805*. PublicAffairs, 2004.

30. Tucker, Spencer. *Stephen Decatur: A Life Most Bold and Daring.* Naval Institute Press, 2005.

31. Ciarrocca, Michelle. "U.S. Arms for

Turkish Abuses." *Mother Jones,* 17 November 1999. www.motherjones.com/politics/1999/11/us-arms-turkish-abuses.

32. Gelvin, James L. *The Modern Middle East: A History*. Oxford University Press, 2011.

33. Gilbert, Martin. *Winston S. Churchill*, Hillsdale College Press, 2011.

34. Chomsky, Noam. *Year 501 The Conquest Continues*. South End Press, 1993.

35. Dell, Jim. *Memorable Quotations from Winston Churchill*. Amazon Digital Services, 2012. www.amazon.com/Memorable-Quotations-Winston-Churchill-Dell-ebook/dp/B00AKF4H-CC.

36. Cleveland, William L. *History of the Modern Middle East*. Westview, 2000.

37. Chomsky, Noam. *Fateful Triangle*. South End Press, 1999.

38. Chomsky, Noam. *Towards a New Cold War*. The New Press New York, 2003.

39. Ibid.

40. "US May soon Become World's Top Oil Producer." *CBS News*, 23 October. 2012, www.cbsnews.com/8301-505123_162-57538431/u.s-may-soon-become-worlds-top-oil-producer/.

41. Ibid.

42. Ibid.

43. "How much oil is consumed in the United States?." *U.S. Energy Information Administration*, 17 March. 2016, www.eia.gov/tools/faqs/faq.cfm?id=33&t=6. Accessed 2 Dec. 2016.

44. Smith, David. "Shell Accused of Fuelling Violence in Nigeria by Paying Rival Militant Gangs." *The Guardian,* 2 October 2011. www.theguardian.com/world/2011/oct/03/shell-accused-of-fuelling-nigeria-conflict.

45. Novak, Matt. "We've Been Incorrectly Predicting Peak Oil For Over a Century." *Gizmodo,* 11 December. 2014, www.paleofuture.gizmodo.com/weve-been-incorrectly-predicting-peak-oil-for-over-a-ce-1668986354. Accessed 2 Jan 2016.

46. Ibid.

47. Clemente, Jude. " How Much Oil Does the World Have Left?" *Forbes,* 25 June. 2015, www.forbes.com/sites/judeclemente/2015/06/25/how-much-oil-does-the-world-have-left/#25d4b-2475dc5. Accessed 2 Jan 2016.

48. Whitney, Lance. "Apple beats world record in quarterly profits." *CNET,* 28 January. 2015, www.cnet.com/news/apple-beats-world-record-in-quarterly-profits-s-p/. Accessed 20 Dec. 2016.

49. Khalidi, Rahsid. *Resurrecting Empire*. Beacon Press, 2004.

50. Ibid.

51.Byrne, Malcolm. "CIA Admits It Was Behind Iran's Coup." *Foreign Policy,* 18 August 2013. www.foreignpolicy.com/articles/2013/08/18/cia_admits_it_was_behind_irans_coup.

52. Stuster, J. Dana. "Maj. Gen. H. Norman Schwarzkopf." *Foreign*

Policy, 20 August 2013. blog.foreignpolicy.com/posts/2013/08/20/the_craziest_detail_about_the_cias_1953_coup_in_iran.

53. Khalidi, Rahsid. *Resurrecting Empire.* Beacon Press, 2004.

54. Yeomans, Jon. " Revealed: the biggest companies in the world in 2016." *The Telegraph,* 20 July 2016. www.telegraph.co.uk/business/2016/07/20/revealed-the-biggest-companies-in-the-world-in-2016/.

55. "BP makes record £17bn profits in 2008 on back of oil surge." *The Telegraph,* 3 February. 2009, www.telegraph.co.uk/finance/newsbysector/energy/4443902/BP-makes-record-17bn-profits-in-2008-on-back-of-oil-surge.html.

56. Abrahamian, Ervand, *Tortured Confessions: Prisons and Public Recantations in Modern Iran* California Press, 1999.

57. "Khosrow Roozbeh." *Critical Montages,* Blogspot, 11 May 2008, montages.blogspot.com/2008/05/khosrow-roozbeh.html. Accessed 12 Dec. 2016.

58. "World: SAVAK: Like the CIA." *Time Magazine,* 19 February. 1979, www.time.com/time/magazine/article/0,9171,912364-1,00.html.

59. "Nation: Nobody Influences Me!" *Time Magazine,* 10 December. 1979, www.time.com/time/magazine/article/0,9171,912545,00.html.

60. Ibid.

61. Ibid.

62. Ibid.

63. Smith, Tony. *America's Mission: The United States and the Worldwide Struggle for Democracy in the Twentieth Century.* Princeton University Press, 1995.

64. "Aryans." *Encyclopaedia Iranica,* www.iranicaonline.org/articles/aryans. Accessed 12 December 2016.

65. Chomsky Noam, *Towards a New Cold War.* The New Press, 2003.

66. Morris, Roger. "Remember: Saddam was our man - A Tyrant 40 Years in the Making." *New York Times,* 14 March 2003. www.nytimes.com/2003/03/14/opinion/a-tyrant-40-years-in-the-making.html?scp=1&sq=sadaam%20morris&st=cse.

67. Ibid.

68. Chandler, Malcolm and Wright, John. *Modern World History.* Oxford: Heinemann Education Publishers, 2001.

69. Bohning, Don. "Assassination plots and schemes: Castro in the crosshairs." *CNN.com,* 19 February. 2008, edition.cnn.com/2008/WORLD/americas/02/19/castro.top10/index.html. Accessed 12 Dec. 2016.

70. Brown, Michael. "The Nationalization of the Iraqi Petroleum Company." *International Journal of Middle East Studies,* vol. 10 no. 1, Feb 1979.

71. Tripp, Charles. *A History of Iraq.* Cambridge, 2002.

72. Ibid.

73. Polk, William R. *Understanding Iraq.* Harper Perennial, 2006.

74. Ibid.

75. Morris, Roger. "Remember: Saddam was our man - A Tyrant 40 Years in the Making." *New York Times,* 14 March 2003. www.nytimes.com/2003/03/14/opinion/a-tyrant-40-years-in-the-making.html?scp=1&sq=sadaam%20morris&st=cse.

76. Aburish, Said. *Saddam Hussein: The Politics of Revenge.* Bloomsbury, 2000.

77. Cockburn, Andrew and Cockburn, Patrick. *Out of the Ashes, The Resurrection of Saddam Hussein.* Harper Perennial, 1999.

78. Lardner, George Jr. "Documents May Give Clues About Obstacles in Hunt for War Criminals." *Washington Post*, 18 March 2001. www.mail-archive.com/ctrl@listserv.aol.com/msg64049.html.

79. Cockburn, Andrew and Cockburn, Patrick. *Out of the Ashes, The Resurrection of Saddam Hussein.* Harper Perennial, 1999.

80. Morris, Roger. "Remember: Saddam was our man - A Tyrant 40 Years in the Making." *New York Times,* 14 March 2003. www.nytimes.com/2003/03/14/opinion/a-tyrant-40-years-in-the-making.html?scp=1&sq=sadaam%20morris&st=cse.

81. Brown, Michael. "The Nationalization of the Iraqi Petroleum Company." *International Journal of Middle East Studies*, vol. 10 no. 1, Feb 1979.

82. Schorr, Daniel. "Telling It Like It Is: Kissinger and the Kurds." *Christian Science Monitor*, 18 October 1996. www.csmonitor.com/1996/1018/101896.opin.

column.1.html.

83. Ibid.

84. Realpolitik, noun, re·al·po·li·tik often capitalized \rā-ˈäl-ˌpō-li-ˌtēk\ "Politics based on practical and material factors rather than on theoretical or ethical objectives." From: www.merriam-webster.com/dictionary/realpolitik.

85. "How Advanced is North Korea's Nuclear Programme?." *BBC News*, 20 May. 2015, www.bbc.com/news/world-asia-pacific-11813699. Accessed 12 Dec. 2016.

86. For a good explanation of Nasserism see "Arab Unity: Nasser's Revolution: In 1952, an Egyptian army officer stepped forward to lead the drive for Arab unity." Al Jazeera, June 20, 2008. www.aljazeera.com/focus/arab ty/2008/02/200852517252821627.html.

87. Cleveland, William L. *History of the Modern Middle East.* Westview, 2000.

88. *The Power of Nightmares.* Directed by Adam Curtis, BBC, 2004.

89. Cleveland, William L and Bunton, Martin. *History of the Modern Middle East.* Westview, 2012.

90. *The Power of Nightmares.* Directed by Adam Curtis, BBC, 2004.

91. Ibid.

92. "Fact Sheet: Extraordinary Rendition." *ACLU*, www.aclu.org/fact-sheet-extraordinary-rendition. Accessed 10 Jan 2017.

93. Donadio, Rachel. "Italy Convicts 23 Americans for C.I.A. Renditions."

New York Times, 4 November 2009. www.nytimes.com/2009/11/05/world/europe/05italy.html?_r=0.

94. Kaminski, Matthew. "Robert Seldon Lady: The Antiterror Spy Left Out in the Cold." *The Wall Street Journal*, 13 September 2013. www.wsj.com/articles/SB1000142412788732457630457907153082314 0604.

95. Donadio, Rachel. "Italy Convicts 23 Americans for C.I.A. Renditions." *New York Times*, 4 November 2009. www.nytimes.com/2009/11/05/world/europe/05italy.html?_r=0.

96. Froomkin, Dan. "New Effort to Rebut Torture Report Undermined as Former Official Admits the Obvious." *The Intercept,* 5 August. 2015, theintercept.com/2015/08/05/new-campaign-rebut-torture-allegations-undermined-former-official-admits-obvious/. Accessed 12 Dec. 2016.

97. Horowitz, Alana. "NYT Will Use The Word Torture, Finally." *Huffington Post,* 7 August. 2014, www.huffingtonpost.com/2014/08/07/nyt-torture_n_5659997.html. Accessed 4 May 2016. Accessed 1 Dec. 2016.

98. Ibid.

99. Hosenball, Mark. "Senate CIA 'Torture' Report Summary To Be Declassified." *Huffington Post,* 29 July. 2014, www.huffingtonpost.com/2014/07/29/senate-cia-torture-report_n_5631984.html. Accessed 4 May 2016.

100. Dilanian, Ken and Sullivan, Eileen. "Associated Press, Colin Powell Initially Kept In The Dark About CIA Interrogation Practices, Report Finds." *Huffington Post,* 30 July. 2014 www.huffingtonpost.com/2014/07/30/colin-powell-cia_n_5635636.html. Accessed 4 Aug 2014.

101. Friedersdorf, Conor. "Dick Cheney Defends the Torture of Innocents." *The Atlantic,* 15 December 2014. www.theatlantic.com/politics/archive/2014/12/dick-cheney-defends-the-torture-innocents/383741/.

102. Hersh, Seymour M. "Selective Intelligence, Donald Rumsfeld has his own special sources. Are they reliable?" *The New Yorker,* 12 May 2003. www.newyorker.com/magazine/2003/05/12/selective-intelligence.

103. Ibid.

104. *The Power of Nightmares.* Directed by Adam Curtis, BBC, 2004.

105. Ibid.

106. "Oil Embargo, 1973–1974,." *U.S. Department of State, Office of the Historian,* history.state.gov/milestones/1969-1976/oil-embargo. Accessed 12 December 2016.

107. Goldschmidt, Arthur Jr. *A Concise History of the Middle East*. Westview, 2002.

108. Cleveland, William L and Bunton, Martin. *History of the Modern Middle East*. Westview, 2012.

109. Chomsky, Noam. *Towards a New Cold War*. The New Press, 2003.

110. Telhami, Shibley. "The Persian Gulf: Understanding the American Oil Strategy." *Brookings,* 1 March. 2002, www.brookings.edu/articles/the-persian-gulf-un-

derstanding-the- ameri-
can-oil-strategy/. Accessed 4 May
2016.

111. Pozzebon, Stefano. "Oil Is Now
Cheaper Than Water." *Business
Insider*, 16 Dec. 2014, www.
businessinsider.com/oil-cheaper-
than-water-2014-12. Accessed 4
May 2016.

112. "Palestinians accuse Israel of 'unfair
distribution' on World Water
Day." *Reuters*, 23 March. 2015,
www.rt.com/news/243081-pal-
estine-water-shortages-israel/.
Accessed 4 May 2016.

"Palestinian water resources are
fully controlled by Israel, subject
to the provisions enshrined in the
Oslo Accords. In the West Bank,
according to some estimates, Israel is using more than 85 percent
of the water, covering around a
quarter of its own needs."

113. Blum, William. *Killing Hope.* Zed
Books, 2014.

114. Ibid.

115. Ibid.

116. Ibid.

117. Ibid.

118. Schivone, Gabriel. "Israel's Proxy
War in Guatemala." *The Journal
of the North American Congress
on Latin America,* nacla.org/
news/2013/4/23/israel
%E2%80%99s-proxy-war-gua-
temala. Accessed 10 December
2016.

119. Ibid.

120. "Ríos Montt on Trial in Guatemala.
A Censored Massacre Made in
USA." *Revolution Newspaper,*

1 May 2013. www.revcom.
us/a/302/a-censored-massacre-
made-in-usa-en.html.

121. Guevara, Ernesto. *Che Guevara
Reader: Writings on Politics &
Revolution*. Ocean Press, 2003.

122. Wines, Michael. "C.I.A. Tie As-
serted in Indonesia Purge." *The
New York Times*, 12 July 1990.
www.nytimes.com/1990/07/12/
world/cia-tie-asserted-in-indo-
nesia-purge.html?pagewant-
ed=all&src=pm.

123. Blum, William. *Rogue State*. Common Courage Press, 2000.

124. Tyler, Andrew. "The life and death
of Victor Jara – a classic feature
from the vaults." *The Guardian,* 18 September 2013. www.
theguardian.com/music/2013/
sep/18/victor-jara-pino-
chet-chile-rocks-backpages.

125. Chomsky, Noam. "An Interview
of Noam Chomsky." Inter-
viewed by David Barsamian.
Secrets, Lies and Democracy,
Odonian Press, 1 5 July 2009.
c h o m s k y - m u s t - r e a d .
b l o g s p o t . c o m / 2 0 0 9 / 0 7 /
s e p t e m b e r - 1 1 - 1 9 7 3 -
c i a - c o u p - i n - c h i l e . h t m -
l # i x z z 3 8 s a 3 S I j D .

126. Ibid.

127. Ibid.

128. "Senate Select Committee to Study
Governmental Operations with
Respect to Intelligence Activ-
ities." *United States Senate,*
www.senate.gov/artandhistory/
history/common/investigations/
ChurchCommittee.htm#Origins.
Accessed 10 Jan 2017.

129. Ibid.

130. Ibid.

131. Ibid.

132. Risen, James and Lichtblaudec, Eric. "Bush Lets U.S. Spy on Callers Without Courts." *New York Times,* 16 December 2005. www.nytimes.com/2005/12/16/politics/bush-lets-us-spy-on-callers-without-courts.html?_r=1.

133. Gellman, Barton, Blake, Aaron, and Miller, Greg. "Edward Snowden comes forward as source of NSA leaks." *Washington Post,* 9 June 2013. www.washingtonpost.com/politics/intelligence-leaders-push-back-on-leakers-media/2013/06/09/fff80160-d122-11e2-a73e-826d299ff459_story.html.

134. "'That's Just Not Done': Merkel Comments on Spying Allegations." *Spiegel online,* 24 October. 2013, www.spiegel.de/international/germany/merkel-comments-on-allegations-the-us-spied-on-her-cell-phone-a-929870.html. Accessed 10 Jan 2017.

135. "Understanding the Iran Contra Affair." *Brown University,* www.brown.edu/Research/Understanding_the_Iran_Contra_Affair/i-the-beginning.php. Accessed 10 Jan 2017.

136. Ibid.

137. Ibid.

138. McManus, Doyle. "Rights Groups Accuse Contras: Atrocities in Nicaragua Against Civilians Charged." *LA Times,* 8 March 1985. articles.latimes.com/1985-03-08/news/mn-32283_1_contras.

139. Ibid.

140. Levin, Marc. "Gary Webb Was Right." *Huffington Post,* 24 Oct. 2014, www.huffingtonpost.com/marc-levin/gary-webb-was-right_b_6024530.html. Accessed 24 Oct 2014.

141. *The Dark Alliance, Gary Webb's Incendiary 1996 SJ Mercury News Exposé.* www.mega.nu/ampp/webb.html. Accessed 10 Jan 2017.

142. Ibid.

143. Levin, Marc. "Gary Webb Was Right." *Huffington Post,* 24 Oct. 2014, www.huffingtonpost.com/marc-levin/gary-webb-was-right_b_6024530.html. Accessed 24 Oct 2014.

144. Ibid.

145. *The Dark Alliance, Gary Webb's Incendiary 1996 SJ Mercury News Exposé.* www.mega.nu/ampp/webb.html. Accessed 10 Jan. 2017.

146. Webb, Gary. *Dark Alliance.* Seven Stories Press, 1998.

147. Cooley, John K. *Unholy Wars.* Pluto Press, 2000.

148. Ibid.

149. Ibid.

150. Ibid.

151. "Assassins." *New World Encyclopedia,* www.newworldencyclopedia.org/entry/Assassins. Accessed 10 Jan 2017.

152. Ibid.

153. Rashid, Ahmed. *Taliban.* Yale, 2000.

154. Sliwinski, Marek. *Afghanistan: The*

Decimation of a People. Orbis, 1989.

155. Cockburn, Alexander And St. Clair, Jeffrey. "How Jimmy Carter and I Started the Mujahideen," *Counterpunch,* 15 Jan. 1998, www. counterpunch.org/1998/01/15/ how-jimmy-carter-and-i-started-the-mujahideen/. Accessed 10 Jan. 2017.

156. Healey, Carrie. "'Chickens come home to roost': Black reactions to JFK's death in 1963." *The Grio,* 22 November. 2013, thegrio. com/2013/11/22/chickens-come-home-to-roost-black-reactions-to-jfks-death-in-1963/ #Duke Ellington's letter of condolence to Jackie Kennedy (JFK Presidential Library). Accessed 10 Jan. 2017.

157. Elliot, Dan. "Colorado Prof Fired After 9-11 Remarks." *The Washington Post,* 24 July 2007. www.washingtonpost.com/wp-dyn/content/article/2007/07/24/ AR2007072402000.html.

158. Adolf Eichmann was former Nazi Officer who was put on trial in Israel in 1960. He was found guilty of war crimes and hanged in 1962.

159. Morson, Berny."CU regents fire Ward Churchill." *Rocky Mountain News*, 25 July 2007. rockymountainnews.com/news/2007/jul/25/ cu-regents-fire-ward-churchill/.

160. Honderich, Ted. *After the Terror.* Edinburgh University Press, 2002.

161. Seidel, Jon. "Hillside Terror Suspect to Judge: 'You arrested me because I'm Muslim.'" *Chicago Sun-Times,* 23 June 2015. chicago.suntimes.com/news/hillside-terror-suspect-to-judge-you-arrested-me-because-im-muslim/ .

162. Howell, Bellan. "Virginia Teen Behind pro-ISIS Twitter account sentence to 11 years." *Washington Times,* 28 Aug 2015. www. washingtontimes.com/news/2015/ aug/28/ali-shukri-amin-va-teen-behind-pro-isis-twitter-ac/.

163. Friedersdorf , Conor. "How Team Obama Justifies the Killing of a 16-Year-Old American." *The Atlantic,* 24 Oct 2012. www. theatlantic.com/politics/archive/2012/10/how-team-obama-justifies-the-killing-of-a-16-year-old-american/264028/.

164. Popular American commentator Fareed Zakaria offers this explanation for the hostility towards the United States from Muslims: "They come out of a culture that reinforces their hostility, distrust and hatred of the West--and of America in particular. This culture does not condone terrorism but fuels the fanaticism that is at its heart. To say that Al Qaeda is a fringe group may be reassuring, but it is false. Read the Arab press in the aftermath of the attacks and you will detect a not-so-hidden admiration for bin Laden." The Politics Of Rage: Why Do They Hate Us? Newsweek, Fareed Zakaria 14 October 2001. This analysis conveniently ignores the long history of intervention and aggression from the military and political leadership of the United States. It also, not surprisingly, gives cover for those policies, since it puts the blame of the "distrust" not on the policies of the Unites States, but on something inherent in the Muslim "world."

165. Blum, William. *Killing Hope.* Zed Books, 2014.

166. Goethe, J.W, Eckermann, J.P. *Con-*

servations with Goethe. Da Capo Press, 1998.

167. Ambrose, Stephen E. and Brinkley, Douglas G. *Rise to Globalism: American Foreign Policy since 1938.* Penguin Press, 1997.

168. Erdbrinkoct, Thomas. "Former American Embassy in Iran Attracts Pride and Dust." *New York Times,* 31 Oct 2013. www.nytimes.com/2013/11/01/world/middleeast/former-american-embassy-in-iran-attracts-pride-and-dust.html?_r=0>.

169. Armstrong, Scott. "Iran Documents Give Rare Glimpse of a CIA Enterprise." *Washington Post,* 31 Jan 1982. nsarchive.files.wordpress.com/2014/05/lexisnexisc2ae-academic_c2a0delivery-status.pdf.

170. Lewis, Neil A., "New Reports Say 1980 Reagan Campaign Tried to Delay Hostage Release." *New York Times,* 15 April 1991. www.nytimes.com/1991/04/15/world/new-reports-say-1980-reagan-campaign-tried-to-delay-hostage-release.html.

173. Wallace, Charles. "Iran, Iraq Still Fail to Bridge Waterway Dispute," *LA Times,* 19 August 1988. articles.latimes.com/1988-08-19/news/mn-739_1_shatt-al-arab.

174. Kurzman, Charles. "Death Tolls of the Iran-Iraq War." *Charles Kurzman,* 31 October. 2013, kurzman.unc.edu/death-tolls-of-the-iran-iraq-war/. Accessed 12 Jan 2017.

175. Garamone, Jim. "Iraq and the Use of Chemical Weapons," *American Forces Press Service,* 23 Jan. 2003, archive.defense.gov/news/newsarticle.aspx?id=29540. Accessed 12 Jan 2017.

176. Harris, Shane and Aid, Matthew M. "CIA Files Prove America Helped Saddam as He Gassed Iran." *Foreign Policy,* 26 Aug 2013. foreignpolicy.com/2013/08/26/exclusive-cia-files-prove-america-helped-saddam-as-he-gassed-iran/.

177. Sciolino, Elaine and Gordon, Michael R. "Confrontation in the Gulf; U.S. Gave Iraq Little Reason Not to Mount Kuwait Assault." *New York Times,* 23 Sept 1990. www.nytimes.com/1990/09/23/world/confrontation-in-the-gulf-us-gave-iraq-little-reason-not-to-mount-kuwait-assault.html.

178. Naar, Ismaeel. "25 years on, Iraq's Kuwait invasion remains a source of bitterness." Al *Arabiya News,* 2 Aug. 2015, english.alarabiya.net/en/perspective/features/2015/08/02/25-years-on-Iraq-s-Kuwait-invasion-remains-a-source-of-bitterness.html. Accessed 10 Jan 2017.

179. Hayes, Thomas C. "Confrontation in the Gulf; The Oilfield Lying Below the Iraq-Kuwait Dispute." *New York Times,* 3 Sept 1990. www.nytimes.com/1990/09/03/world/confrontation-in-the-gulf-the-oilfield-lying-below-the-iraq-kuwait-dispute.html.

180. "Iraq Accuses Kuwait Again." *CBS News,* 14 Sept. 2000, www.cbsnews.com/news/iraq-accuses-kuwait-again/. Accessed 10 Jan 2017.

181. Falk, Richard, Gendzier, Irene, and Lifton, Robert Jay, editors. *Crimes of War Iraq.* Nation Books, 2006.

182. Ibid.

183. Arnove, Anthony, editor. *Iraq Under Siege*. South End Press, 2000.

184. Falk, Richard, Gendzier, Irene, and Lifton, Robert Jay, editors. *Crimes of War Iraq*. Nation Books, 2006.

185. "Defense Policy Guidance." *Frontline,* PBS, www.pbs.org/wgbh/pages/frontline/shows/iraq/etc/wolf.html. Accessed 10 Jan 2017.

186. Ibid.

187. "World's Largest Economies." *CNN Money*, money.cnn.com/news/economy/world_economies_gdp/index.html. Accessed 10 Jan 2017.

188. Diaz, Jesus. "China used more concrete in 3 years than the US in 100 years." *Gizmodo/Sploid,* 22 Feb. 2015, sploid.gizmodo.com/china-used-more-concrete-in-3-years-than-the-us-in-100-1687311350. Accessed 10 Jan 2017.

189. "Saddam's Iraq: Key Events." *BBC,* news.bbc.co.uk/2/shared/spl/hi/middle_east/02/iraq_events/html/ground_war.stm. Accessed 10 Jan 2017.

190. DeGhett Torie Rose, "The War Photo No One Would Publish." *The Atlantic,* 8 Aug 2014. www.theatlantic.com/international/archive/2014/08/the-war-photo-no-one-would-publish/375762/.

191. Crispin Miller, Mark. "A Lesson In U.S. Propaganda." *AlterNet,* 2 Jan. 2003, www.alternet.org/story/14877/a_lesson_in_u.s._propaganda. Accessed 10 Jan 2017.

192. "Wag the Dog" (1997) was a film made about a fictional American president who orchestrated a conflict to distract the media and public from a scandal.

193. Shelton, Hugh. *Without Hesitation: The Odyssey of an American Warrior.* St. Martin's Griffin, 2011.

194. Ibid.

195. Churchill, Ward. *On the Justice of Roosting Chickens*, AK Press, 2003.

196. Ibid.

197. Cohen, David. "Hidden Treasures." *Slate.com*, 6 Feb. 2003, www.slate.com/articles/news_and_politics/the_gist/2003/02/hidden_treasures.html. Accessed 10 Jan 2017.

198. Bishara, Marwan. "ISIL, CIA, Mossad, Quds Force, etc." *Al Jazeera* 26 Feb. 2015, www.aljazeera.com/indepth/opinion/2015/02/daesh-cia-mossad-quds-force-150226052024592.html. Accessed 10 Jan 2017.

199. Massad, Joseph. "The Future of the Arab Uprisings." *Al Jazeera,* 18 May. 2011, www.aljazeera.com/indepth/opinion/2011/05/201151885013738898.html. Accessed 10 Jan 2017.

200. Lehren, Andrew W, and Shane, Scott. "Leaked Cables Offer Raw Look at U.S. Diplomacy." *New York Times*. 28 November 2010. www.nytimes.com/2010/11/29/world/29cables.html.

201. Zenko, Micah. "Clear and Present Safety: The United States Is More Secure than Washington Thinks." *Council on Foreign Relations,* 23 February. 2012, blogs.cfr.org/zenko/2012/02/23/clear-and-present-safety-the-united-states-is-more-secure-than-washington-thinks/.

202. Ibid.

203. Tharoor, Ishaan. "Saudi Arabia passes Russia as world's third biggest military." *Washington Post,* 5 April 2016. www.washingtonpost.com/news/worldviews/wp/2016/04/05/saudi-arabia-passes-russia-as-worlds-third-biggest-military-spender/?utm_term=.f4435f831b65.

204. Ibid.

205. Ibid.

206. McGreal, Chris. "Palestinians hit by sonic boom air raids." *The Guardian,* 3 November 2005. www.theguardian.com/world/2005/nov/03/israel.

207. Davies, Nicolas J.S. "The Record U.S. Military Budget, *The Huffington Post,* 2 October. 2015, m.huffpost.com/us/entry/8227820. Accessed 10 Jan 2017.

208. Shakespeare, William. "Macbeth," Dover, 1993.

209. Hannah Arendt was an important 20th century intellectual and philosopher. She attended Adolph Eichmann's trial in Israel and used the term "the banality of evil" to describe him.

210. Arendt, Hannah. *The Origins of Totalitarianism.* Harcourt, 1973.

211. "Report: U.S.-Led Strikes In Iraq And Syria Killed Hundreds Of Civilians." *Huffington Post,* 3 Aug. 2015, www.huffingtonpost.com/entry/us-airstrikes-civilian-casualties_55bf6f79e4b0d4f33a034505. Accessed 10 Aug 2015.

212. Pinker, Steven and Mack, Andrew. "The World Is Not Falling Apart." *Slate.com,* 22 December. 2014, www.slate.com/articles/news_and_politics/foreigners/2014/12/the_world_is_not_falling_apart_the_trend_lines_reveal_an_increasingly_peaceful.html. Accessed 10 Jan 2017.

213. Ibid.

ALSO BY TOUFIC EL RASSI
ARAB IN AMERICA

Arab in America is the eye-opening story of the life of an average Arab-American struggling with his identity in an increasingly hostile nation. Using the graphic novel as his medium, Lebanon-born author Toufic El Rassi chronicles his experience growing up Arab in America. Keen observations, clever insights and painful honesty make El Rassi's work shine as a critical 21st century memoir.

From childhood through adolescence, and as an adult, El Rassi illustrates the prejudice and discrimination Arabs and Muslims experience in American society. He contends with ignorant teachers, racist neighbors, bullying classmates, and a growing sense of alienation. El Rassi recounts his personal experiences after the 9/11 attacks and during the implementation of new security and immigration laws that followed.

El Rassi gives context to current world events, providing readers with an overview of the modern history of the Middle East, including the Gulf wars. He also examines the roles American films and news media play in creating negative stereotypes of Arab-Americans, showing how difficult it is to have an Arab identity in a society saturated with anti-Arab images and messages.

ARAB IN AMERICA
BY TOUFIC EL RASSI
120 PAGES • 7 x 11 • $14.95
ISBN 978-0-86719-673-3
PUBLISHED BY LAST GASP
www.lastgasp.com

"Complex and rewarding"
—*The Guardian*

"Pen power...Tackles fear, anger, and history"
—*The Wall Street Journal*

In this autobiography meets graphic novel, Beirut-born lecturer and writer Toufic El Rassi illustrates the daily prejudice and discrimination experienced by Muslims and Arabs in modern American society. Drawing from his own personal history, Toufic shows how hard it is to maintain an Arab identity in a country saturated with anti-Arab propaganda, and he examines the role of media and pop culture against the backdrop of 9/11, two Gulf Wars and U.S. involvement in the Middle East. Hilarious, enraging and poignantly relevant!